FLYING BLIND

Flying Blind

A play by

Bill Morrison

FABER & FABER
London Boston

First published in 1978
by Faber and Faber Limited
3 Queen Square London WC1N 3AU
Printed in Great Britain by
Latimer Trend & Company Ltd Plymouth

British Library Cataloguing in Publication Data

Morrison, Bill
Flying blind.
I. Title
822'9'14 PR6063.0/

ISBN 0-571-11304-4 Pbk.

CHARACTERS

DAN POOTS, a medical representative, in his thirties
LIZ POOTS, his wife, the same age
MICHAEL, a friend of theirs from London, same age
BOYD, a lawyer, same age
BERTHA, their next-door neighbour, about forty
CAROL, a student, nineteen
SMYTH, a workman, middle-aged
TULLY, a young workman
MAC, leader of a Protestant gang
SHORTY, a member of the gang
MAGOO, a member of the gang
BILLY, a member of the gang, fifteen
UNA, a young IRA volunteer
SEAN, a young IRA volunteer

The setting is a house in Belfast in the present.

Flying Blind was first performed at the Everyman Theatre, Liverpool, on 16th November 1977, with the following cast:

DAN POOTS	Paul Jesson
LIZ POOTS	Valerie Lilley
MICHAEL	David Fielder
BOYD	Philip Donaghy
BERTHA	Anne-Louise Wakefield
CAROL	Victoria Hardcastle
SMYTH	George Costigan
TULLY	Chris Darwin
MAC	Paul Harmon
SHORTY	George Costigan
MAGOO	Chris Darwin
BILLY	Chris Fairbank
UNA	Gerry McAlpine
SEAN	Chris Fairbank

The play was directed by Chris Bond

ACT ONE

The living-room of a large three-storey terrace house in the university district of Belfast. It is two rooms knocked into one, imaginatively furnished with a mixture of modern and old furnishings. There is a large stereo, a lot of books; the impression is not rich but comfortable and cultivated. There is some clutter to indicate a small child and a Wendy House to one side. In a side wall, towards the front, is the entrance from the hall, stairs and front door, none of which are seen. In the same wall, at the back, is the door of a walk-in cloakroom. Beside it, in the back wall, is the entrance to the kitchen. At the opposite end of the back wall there are sliding glass doors leading to a white-painted yard full of potted plants, which screen most of the yard from view. People coming into the yard from the back alley can enter through the kitchen or by the glass doors. It is a sunny Saturday morning.

LIZ POOTS *enters from the kitchen. She is an attractive, organized woman in her thirties. She carries two pieces of toast. Opens cloakroom and takes out a light overcoat, closes door. Juggles toast and coat, puts toast on back of an armchair, puts on coat, knocks down a piece of toast, lifts it, has to find somewhere to clean her hand, hesitates, uses back of chair. She casts an eye over the room, picks up an empty whiskey bottle, then reconsiders and puts it down. Goes to door to hall. Calls quietly up the stairs.*

LIZ: Rosy. Rosy. Aren't you ready yet? Come on, love, we have to hurry, you don't want to be late for your class. And be quiet. Nobody else is up yet. Don't waken Daddy or Michael. Hurry up now, I'll get the car started. And remember to close the front door when you come out.

(LIZ *takes a last look round then exits. A pause. Then the living-room door is pulled closed by the unseen* ROSY. *No sound of the front door closing.*

A short pause. The living-room door opens and MICHAEL *enters. He is also in his thirties, tousled, just out of bed, wearing jeans and a T-shirt, long-haired. He is hungover, still half-asleep. He shivers, feels a radiator, which is cold, then goes into the kitchen. Leaves door open.*

After a moment a head in a flat cap appears round the door, then another head. SMYTH, *a small middle-aged man in working overalls, comes cautiously in, followed by* TULLY, *larger and younger, who carries a tool-bag. They are very cautious.* MICHAEL *walks out of the kitchen. All start back in shock at seeing each other.* MICHAEL *retreats towards the middle of the room,* SMYTH *and* TULLY *back up. Stare at each other.)*

MICHAEL: (*Nervous, too loud*) What do you want?

SMYTH: It's all right, Tully, he's English. That means he's not robbing the place.

TULLY: Are you sure?

MICHAEL: I'm not English, actually.

SMYTH: Oh.

MICHAEL: How did you get in here?

SMYTH: The front door was open.

TULLY: I rang the bell.

MICHAEL: I don't think it works.

TULLY: Then you didn't hear it.

SMYTH: Are you . . . like, are you the owner?

MICHAEL: No. I've just arrived myself. What do you want? Money?

SMYTH: No.

TULLY: We're here for the unit.

MICHAEL: The unit? What unit?

SMYTH: The unit in the kitchen.

(*They all look at the kitchen. There is a sudden loud metallic sound from in there.)*

MICHAEL: What do you want here?

SMYTH: (*Putting his hands up*) Nothing. Nothing, mister. Tell your mate in the kitchen to take it easy.

MICHAEL: I don't know who's in there.

SMYTH: Neither do I.

MICHAEL: You said it was your unit.

SMYTH: I meant the central heating unit. We're from the Gas Board.

(*They all look at the kitchen.* MICHAEL *takes a deep breath and walks into the kitchen, turns and walks straight out again.*)

MICHAEL: It was the pop-up toaster, it popped. I was making breakfast when you came in.

SMYTH: You mean you live here?

MICHAEL: I'm staying here.

SMYTH: Why didn't you say so?

TULLY: You should keep the front door locked.

SMYTH: You never know what you might find in our job.

TULLY: It was lying open, that's why we came in.

SMYTH: This is Belfast.

TULLY: Anything can happen.

MICHAEL: I'm sorry, I'm afraid I jumped to conclusions, too. I thought you had broken in, or were collecting money for some organization or something.

TULLY: Not up here.

MICHAEL: Why not?

TULLY: This is round the university. Posh. Not much trouble here.

SMYTH: God, you put the heart across me. Sometimes I think I'll never go through an open door again without a signed paper telling me what's on the other side.

MICHAEL: I really am sorry.

TULLY: I'll away and close the front door. This is Belfast.

(TULLY *goes out. Door closed.* SMYTH *produces work-sheet.*)

SMYTH: How long has the central heating been off?

MICHAEL: I don't know.

(TULLY *comes back.*)

TULLY: Have you no bars on that door?

MICHAEL: I . . . I don't know.

TULLY: It only has the one lock.

SMYTH: Tully, away into the kitchen and have a look at the unit.

TULLY: Right.

(TULLY *exits to kitchen.*)

SMYTH: Is your name Poots?

MICHAEL: No, that's Dan, he owns the house. He's still in bed. I'm a friend of his.
SMYTH: You don't know much about the place.
MICHAEL: I only arrived last night.
SMYTH: You're from England?
MICHAEL: No.
SMYTH: Oh.
MICHAEL: That is, yes, I am.
SMYTH: Oh.
MICHAEL: I live there, I came from there, to here, but I'm not from there.
SMYTH: Oh.
MICHAEL: I'm from here.
SMYTH: Oh.
MICHAEL: I mean, I was born here.
SMYTH: (*Light dawns*) Ohh. You don't sound like it. You've lost the accent.
MICHAEL: It's a good few years since I lived here.
SMYTH: Lucky for you.
MICHAEL: I suppose so.
SMYTH: Still, things aren't always as bad as they seem. Look at you.
MICHAEL: What?
SMYTH: With the long hair and the jeans and all I thought you were in here after the colour telly. Saturday morning's a favourite time, you know. People asleep or out shopping.
MICHAEL: Would they take the risk in daylight?
SMYTH: Who's to stop them? Keep your mouth shut and claim the insurance, you live longer. Who would say boo to them? Only mugs like me.
MICHAEL: The police . . .
SMYTH: The polis is too busy elsewhere.
MICHAEL: What about the Army?
SMYTH: I was coming to work this morning on the bus. It's packed. There's not many buses left to run up our way. The Army stopped it, get on, look at everybody, make their check, and as they're getting off this big British sergeant stops and looks round at all of us sitting there and he says,

'Cheer up,' he says, 'have you all forgotten how to smile, for Chrissake?' Smile! Can you beat that?

MICHAEL: I don't quite understand.

SMYTH: If you want people to smile you don't send in the fucking Army. Do you?

MICHAEL: Ah . . . I was making some coffee, would you like some?

SMYTH: That's very civil of you.

(MICHAEL *and* SMYTH *go into the kitchen.* DAN POOTS *enters through the living-room door. In his thirties. Wears only a towelling robe. He has his eyes closed and his hands stretched out before him as if sleep-walking. In one hand he carries his underwear. He walks across the room, hits a chair.*)

DAN: Shit.

(DAN *opens his eyes, rubs his foot. Lays his clothes out on an armchair and plugs in an electric fire to warm them. Arranged so as to be masked from the kitchen. He then points himself at the door, eyes closed, arms out-stretched, and goes towards it. The door is edge on to him so his arms pass on either side and he collides with it.*)

DAN: Bloody hell.

(DAN *exits.* MICHAEL, *worried, enters and takes a look round, followed by* SMYTH. *Both have mugs of coffee and* SMYTH *a plate of biscuits.* SMYTH *goes to armchair, looks surprised, then shrugs, dumps the clothes in the back of the chair, gets ready to settle down.* MICHAEL *has to use two shaky hands to drink his coffee.*)

SMYTH: Heavy night last night?

MICHAEL: I'm afraid so.

SMYTH: I know the feeling.

MICHAEL: To tell you the truth, I don't remember much about it. I'd had a few before I even got on the plane.

SMYTH: Afraid of flying? I'm the same. I think if we were meant to fly we'd grow wings.

MICHAEL: No, I was afraid of landing. Landing here.

SMYTH: Not been back for a good while?

MICHAEL: It's like a trip back in time. It's very hard to start again.

SMYTH: You'll see plenty of changes. D'y'smoke?

(MICHAEL *shakes his head,* SMYTH *settles in the chair and lights up.*)

MICHAEL: All I can compare the city to is the pictures of Berlin after the war.

SMYTH: Oh no. That's all urban re-development.

MICHAEL: What?

SMYTH: That's the name for it. The boys provide free demolition, then there's insurance and the government compensation. Great racket. Of course, when the city starts re-building who do you think's intimidating off all the competition and picking up the next fat wad of the taxpayers' money to build the next lot of vertical slums? You've guessed it—the boys.

MICHAEL: It is one version of owning the means of production.

SMYTH: Honest to God, there are days when I waken up and then I say to myself, that was a stupid thing to do, you know. But I don't bother, I just do my job.

MICHAEL: But, being serious, don't you think it's essential that both sides, I mean the working class, must get together here, that any solution must come from them?

SMYTH: I'm not working class, I've got a job. The working class is all on the dole.

MICHAEL: Well, of course, economic exploitation is one of the root causes of division.

SMYTH: There's plenty of money about. It comes out of my pocket, and yours. You can't help but waken up sometimes. There's all these boys running around trying their best to blow my arse to the moon—and I'm paying them to do it. If they're not drawing the dole they get thousands in compensation. It's a queer kind of revolution when the government finances it. Do you know how much a knee-capping is worth?

MICHAEL: No.

SMYTH: About 400 quid. There's plenty of fly boys . . . you just put a bullet through the fleshy bit at the back of the leg there, then hop down on your National Health crutches and collect. It's one way of raising the fare to England. And muggins here is paying. Where did you come from, London?

MICHAEL: Yes.
SMYTH: What do they think of us over there? I suppose they don't understand it.
MICHAEL: Do you?
SMYTH: No.
MICHAEL: Then you can't blame them.
SMYTH: Why not? I used to be British and proud of it, now I'm just British, that is until the British bugger off.
MICHAEL: Wouldn't that bring people together?
SMYTH: Aye, at High Noon, for the big show-down. It wasn't Willie Whitelaw we needed, it was the Lone Ranger.
MICHAEL: But bringing in more troops, more force, can never lead to a solution.
SMYTH: This is only practice. The big one is still to come. I mean, it's everywhere, isn't it? Everyone is taking to the gun to get what they want. Here it happens to be Protestant and Catholic, or Loyalist and Republican, or whatever you want to call it, but it's everywhere. Them and us. It's about a fella pointing a gun at you and saying, you will do what I want you to, or else—bang.
MICHAEL: But both sides are at that here, both armed, both threatening, both wrong.
SMYTH: And I'm in the middle. Muggins again. And that's not even counting the fellas that just want to rob me.
MICHAEL: My point is this isn't a simple confrontation of the State and terrorism. Both sides are trapped in violence. There have to be other forms of action.
SMYTH: Such as?
MICHAEL: Well . . . radical political action.
SMYTH: What am I going to say to this fella? This is a radical political action I have here pointed at you, drop your gun? Are you one of those Marxists?
MICHAEL: No, I lecture in Sociology.
SMYTH: Do you teach your students about revolution?
MICHAEL: That is part of the curriculum, but only a small part.
SMYTH: You'll soon be teaching the buggers self-defence.
MICHAEL: I try to teach them . . . no, I try to help them . . . to understand reality, the reality of social forces, I want them

to think for themselves, to ask questions, to cut through the lies and evasions, to look for truth.

SMYTH: You see the students here? They started it all back in 1969. Protest marches. It was fashionable. Mind you, they had a case. But there were still rules then, a referee, you could get off-side. Now, there is not one student to be seen on the rimrock. I don't blame them. They have the chance to get out. Like you.

MICHAEL: I left long before the troubles.

SMYTH: There's nobody left up in Comanche Territory, except the Comanches.

(TULLY *enters from the kitchen.*)

MICHAEL: What's Comanche Territory?

SMYTH: Round about the Upper Falls. Tully lives up there. Don't you, Tully? Have a bicky, Tull.

TULLY: Aye, up on the reservation.

SMYTH: Are you married?

MICHAEL: I was . . . that is . . . well, I am . . . sort of.

(SMYTH *and* TULLY *exchange a look of incomprehension.*)

SMYTH: Any kids?

MICHAEL: I'm afraid not, no, we had no family.

SMYTH: Tully has the one wee girl, he lives for that wee girl. She's awful bright. Tell him about her, Tully.

TULLY: She screams in the night now. Mammy, she screams, don't let them come for me. (*Proudly shows a photo from his wallet.*)

MICHAEL: What age is she?

TULLY: Seven.

MICHAEL: My God, what do you do?

TULLY: The wife got her some pills off the doctor. The same as the ones she takes for her nerves. She's quiet now. Smithy, I can't see how to fix this.

SMYTH: Have another look.

TULLY: It won't ignite.

(TULLY *exits into kitchen.*)

SMYTH: (*Calling after him*) Just make sure you don't blow us up. (*Then low tone.*) Tully's a Catholic. You're not a Catholic, are you?

MICHAEL: No.
SMYTH: No, you don't have the look. You can tell.
MICHAEL: Religion never made sense to me.
SMYTH: Tully and I have been together on this job five years now. Never had a hard word. Mind you, he never says much. A grand lad, does everything I tell him. I've nothing against Catholics. As individuals. In fact, I used to think that I didn't care one way or another about a person's religion. Religion to me was just having somebody to bury you. Jesus, I wasn't far off the mark at that. But when I look back, I was living in noddyland. You see . . . it's in you, bred in you.
MICHAEL: You mean the tribal history.
SMYTH: I mean that what you are up against here are one hundred proof banana-heads. They're not all there. I should know, I'm one of them.
MICHAEL: You?
SMYTH: Oh not now. I don't belong to nothing, never did. But you soon remember what foot you dig with when the kicking starts. I only did the one thing, and that was away back at the beginning, but it will illustrate to you that the first thing that flies out of the window is not your bum but your brains. Let me tell you. Here I am, working for the Gas, wife and kids, terrace house, mixed area, mostly Protestant, no bother. This is 'sixty-nine. There'd been riots up the Falls, all that going on. And all these stories are flying about about how the Catholics were going to come down and get us. I wish to Christ I knew where those stories started and who started them and what they got out of it. It's what my Da always said, look for the man who stands to make a profit.
MICHAEL: That was the sort of thing that used to happen before an election.
SMYTH: Maybe it was the same fellas then. Anyway, this night we're all standing out at our front gates. The women and children are locked in the house. All I'm thinking about is defending my home. People are excited, rumours going round, and this is where you start remembering all the stories about all the previous troubles. This is where yours

truly and the whole street is beginning to slip a gear. And a couple of ganches are trying to organize us into vigilantes. They're drunk, looking for trouble, fellas on the dole with nothing better to do. Ed the Ted. I know for a fact he only worked one day in the last ten years and that was the day he hurt his back. Now he walks round the Shankhill with four bodyguards, but that's another story.

MICHAEL: And were you attacked?

SMYTH: That's the story. This fella suddenly comes racing down the road. 'They're coming, they're coming,' he shouts. Now I will tell you no word of a lie, I do not remember what happened next. That's hard to believe.

MICHAEL: I believe you. It can happen.

SMYTH: The next thing I do remember is three o'clock in the morning knocking on the back door of our house. The wife let me in. Our street hadn't been touched, they hadn't been coming for us at all. Mind you, they've made up for it since. I was covered in dirt, I had one sleeve burnt away, and I was carrying a big iron bar. The missus says, 'In the name of God, what have you been up to?' I told her. I don't know. It must have been anaemia, or whatever you call it.

MICHAEL: Amnesia.

SMYTH: I'd flipped my fucking wig. What did I discover the next morning? We had burned down over one hundred Catholic homes. Nobody was killed, but I wouldn't have known if I had. I was not guilty while the absence of mind was disturbed, but I did it. Why? The way I see it, it was three hundred years of history bursting, right?

MICHAEL: Yes, I think it was.

SMYTH: Well, then after that the British troops came in and built the Peace Line and then the real war started. Now, what does that make me?

MICHAEL: A victim, I think.

SMYTH: I've got two lads. I never see them. One of them was lifted, took away for a while. He's back now. I never ask him. He would kick the shit out of me as quick as look at me. He thinks I'm a failure because I stopped. Now, you're an educated man. What do I do?

MICHAEL: Well . . . it's very difficult of course to give a full answer. . . .

SMYTH: The storm is raging. Do I put my head down and ride it out? Will it just come back? What if I get up tomorrow and the roof and the walls are gone, nothing left at all? Did I, muggins, deserve that? That, pal, is the question of the century.

MICHAEL: I am sure it is not insoluble.

SMYTH: See you fellas, you talk about five years, ten, the future. I'm going out for a drink tonight and I have a fifty-fifty chance of getting back alive. What do I do?

MICHAEL: I don't know.

SMYTH: (*Laughs gleefully*) I buy a fucking bazooka, eh?

(TULLY *appearing from the kitchen hears this. Looks at* MICHAEL *and also laughs.*)

TULLY: I can't seem to get this to work.

SMYTH: Let's have a look, Tully, my son. You might need a part out of the van.

(SMYTH *and* TULLY *exit to kitchen, chuckling.* MICHAEL *shakes his head, then gathers cups and plate and follows them.* DAN, *off-stage, comes downstairs, opens front door, then enters, normally this time. Carries rest of his clothes. Has to rescue his underwear from back of the chair, then, warming them quickly, picks up underpants, loosens his robe, ready to begin dressing.* TULLY *enters.*)

TULLY: Ah . . . excuse me.

(DAN *spins round, covers his genitals.*)

DAN: The TV isn't insured.

TULLY: Wha'?

(MICHAEL *enters.*)

MICHAEL: Dan, good morning.

TULLY: I'm just, like, going out to the van.

(TULLY *goes out living-room door.*)

DAN: Who's he?

MICHAEL: He's from the Gas Board.

DAN: Oh.

(TULLY *puts his head in again.*)

TULLY: Somebody's opened the front door again.

DAN: Leave it open.
TULLY: OK.
(TULLY *exits.*)
DAN: Who closed the door?
MICHAEL: Well, we did.
DAN: Leave it open.
MICHAEL: Do you think that's wise?
DAN: This is a free country. Leave all the doors open.
MICHAEL: Are you sober?
DAN: I'm cold.
MICHAEL: I got a hell of a shock earlier. They just walked in on me.
(DAN *ignores this. Wants to dress but doesn't want to be interrupted.*)
Well, I'm just popping up to the loo. Coffee's hot.
(MICHAEL *goes out to go upstairs.* DAN *turns to rewarm his underpants, ready to put them on.*
SMYTH *enters.*)
SMYTH: I always say it's not the same without a fire.
DAN: (*Spinning round*) What?
SMYTH: You can't beat a good fire.
DAN: This is a smokeless zone.
SMYTH: You need the central heating.
DAN: Who are you?
SMYTH: I'm the Gas. But nothing cheers you up like a good fire. My mother always said she could see the future in the flames.
DAN: I had a dream last night. About a cat. A big black cat. It was blind. It had no eyes. It jumped up on my shoulder, and then it walked round the back of my head swishing its tail, walked back and forth, and then it sat down on my left shoulder and began to whisper in my ear. I said, 'Who are you? What do you want?' It said, 'I have come to take you on a journey, don't be afraid. I have come to comfort you.' Now what sort of a conversation is that, even for a cat?
SMYTH: I can't stand cats.
DAN: I don't remember dreams. I can't forget this one.
SMYTH: Sounds like a nightmare to me.

DAN: No, it wasn't. There is an explanation. I have a friend that has a blind black cat. Called Pluto.

SMYTH: Pluto?

(TULLY *enters with a part.*)

DAN: The cat, not the friend. Pluto.

TULLY: Was he not the dog? The dog in Mickey Mouse? I've got this to try. (*Showing part to* SMYTH.)

SMYTH: We'll see if it works.

TULLY: I like cartoons.

(SMYTH *and* TULLY *go into kitchen.* DAN *turns to stereo, switches on.*)

DAN: I must have some Charlie Parker.

(MICHAEL *enters, interrupts him.*)

MICHAEL: Have you heard the news?

DAN: What news?

MICHAEL: The news.

DAN: What's happened?

MICHAEL: I don't know. Didn't you hear?

DAN: Hear what?

MICHAEL: The news. On the radio.

DAN: Oh that. I don't listen to that.

MICHAEL: But you must listen to the news.

DAN: Why?

MICHAEL: To know what is happening. In London I'm glued to the bulletins to hear anything about Ulster.

DAN: I play my records.

MICHAEL: You mean you don't listen at all?

DAN: It's always the same.

MICHAEL: New incidents are happening every day. The situation is changing all the time.

DAN: Beep. Beep. Beep. Here is the Northern Ireland News. The latest scoreline is Protestants 720; Catholics 992. Four bombs, three murders, a tar and feathering; a statement in Parliament that it is only a matter of time before the Army defeats terrorism; Paisley says NO!—he hadn't heard the question but he knows the answer; an ex-Unionist MP says it is all a red plot financed by Moscow, and he's opening a new restaurant. PS Three more British-owned factories have closed and unemployment in selected areas is over 40 per cent. The situation is changing all the time.

MICHAEL: You know that isn't what I meant.

DAN: Do you still like Charlie Parker?

MICHAEL: It has to be reported. We need the information. We need to understand.

DAN: What good does it do me to know all that?

MICHAEL: What possible good will living in ignorance do you?

DAN: I just try to live through another day.

MICHAEL: I'm sorry, I didn't mean that the way it sounded. It's too early in the morning. My God, we shifted a few last night. Did I say anything stupid?

DAN: (*Considering*) No.

MICHAEL: I was . . . in a bit of a state . . . coming back.

DAN: Why did you come back?

MICHAEL: It was good to see you again.

DAN: Yes. It was.

MICHAEL: Where's Liz?

DAN: She'll have taken Rosy to her dancing class. It's a kids' class on Saturday mornings.

MICHAEL: How are you and Liz getting on?

(*By now* DAN *has a record on. He deliberately puts on his headphones and plugs them in.*)

Would you like some coffee? (*No answer.*) I'll make some coffee.

(MICHAEL *goes into the kitchen.* DAN, *still listening, edges to the end of the headphone lead and manages to grab his underpants. About to put them on when* LIZ *enters from hall.*)

LIZ: Who left the front door open? Dan? Dan. I think I should learn sign language.

DAN: (*Slips headphones down*) What?

LIZ: The front door was left open.

DAN: Good.

LIZ: Anybody could come in.

DAN: I'm only standing here naked.

LIZ: We need bolts and chains.

DAN: (*Regarding his prick*) It won't attack anybody.

LIZ: Don't I know it.

DAN: Let's not start that.
LIZ: I wouldn't mind. I wouldn't mind starting something.
DAN: Now?
LIZ: I mean bolts and chains for the door.
DAN: No.
(TULLY *enters.* DAN *covers himself.* LIZ *jumps when he speaks.*)
TULLY: Oh, excuse me.
LIZ: Good God.
TULLY: I got the wrong part.
(TULLY *goes outside.*)
LIZ: Amateur theatricals?
DAN: The Gas Board.
LIZ: Oh good, I thought they'd forgotten us. Is Michael awake?
(MICHAEL *enters with a mug of coffee.*)
MICHAEL: Liz. How are you? Good morning. (*Kisses her cheek.*) You look terrific.
LIZ: Thank you.
MICHAEL: Here's coffee.
LIZ: How thoughtful of you. Just as I come in.
MICHAEL: Back in a moment.
(MICHAEL *goes back into kitchen.*)
DAN: That was mine.
LIZ: What?
DAN: That coffee.
LIZ: If you're desperate, have it.
DAN: No.
LIZ: Michael's probably getting you one.
(*Enter* TULLY.)
TULLY: It's all right. I've got a new part.
LIZ: Oh good.
(TULLY *goes through to kitchen.*)
The Bionic Man?
(*There is a crash from the kitchen of breaking crockery.* MICHAEL *comes out.*)
MICHAEL: Sorry. Sorry, Dan, that was your coffee. Don't worry, Liz, I'll clear it up. I'll bring you one in a moment. I'm talking to the other workman. Fascinating.
(MICHAEL *goes back into kitchen.*)

LIZ: What other one?

DAN: He watches the big one working.

LIZ: As long as they do the job. Did you hear the news this morning? A hundred and sixty-four people were killed in a plane crash.

(DAN *puts his headphones on again.*)

I wonder which mug he broke? Oh . . .

(LIZ *searches among books and papers, finds a sheet of foolscap which is painted a uniform red on both sides and brings it over to hold before* DAN. *He takes off headphones.*)

DAN: What is it?

LIZ: A present for you. Rosy painted it. She's been keeping it for you for days but either she's in bed when you get home or you're in bed when she goes out.

DAN: I said hello to her this morning.

LIZ: Yes, but you lay and wouldn't open your eyes.

DAN: I was blind.

LIZ: Can you see now?

DAN: I'm afraid so.

LIZ: Well, what do you think?

DAN: What's it a picture of?

LIZ: A snowball. That's what she told me.

DAN: A snowball is round.

LIZ: That's what I said. She looked at me as if I was daft.

DAN: A snowball is white.

LIZ: Do you know what she said to that? I know that, Mummy, I coloured it red because I had no white paint. (DAN *begins to laugh.*) She's not very bright sometimes.

DAN: She may be a genius.

LIZ: Anyway, it's her present for you.

DAN: We'll call it—Portrait of Paisley.

(DAN *goes and pins it up.*)

LIZ: Will I tell her you said thank you?

DAN: I'll tell her myself.

LIZ: When?

DAN: Today.

LIZ: Won't you be out drinking today?

DAN: I dreamt about Derek's black cat last night. He sat on my shoulder. He wasn't just blind, he had no eyes, and he whispered to me, all about death.

LIZ: It's always the opposite of what we dream that happens. Isn't it? Put the record off, I want to talk to you.

DAN: It's Bird. It's Charlie Parker.

LIZ: Please, Dan.

DAN: I always play Bird on Saturday mornings.

(*Enter* MICHAEL.)

MICHAEL: I don't think they know how to fix your central heating. Sorry, Dan, I forgot your coffee. Liz, did you get the newspapers when you were out?

LIZ: We have the *Guardian* delivered.

MICHAEL: Don't you get the local papers? I want to see them all. I'll get dressed and go down to the paper shop.

LIZ: Do you want to use my car?

MICHAEL: I can walk.

LIZ: It's probably simpler. I got stopped by the Army this morning.

MICHAEL: What happened?

LIZ: It was just routine. They're a new lot, we haven't had them in our area before.

DAN: (*Sarcastic*) Great.

MICHAEL: Does that matter?

DAN: It means I'll have to go through the same explanations all over again. 'Are you travelling on business, sir?' 'Yes.' 'What is your business, sir?' 'I am a drug pusher.' Pause. 'Open the boot of your car, sir.' 'Bloody' ell, what are these?' Then I produce the card and say, 'I am a medical representative, I am a supplier of happy pills.' And do you know what they always say—'Oh look, those are the ones I take. I hope you sell plenty of those tranquillizers, mate, it might help to keep the buggers quiet.'

MICHAEL: Don't you worry about him having to drive everywhere? (*Sees* LIZ'*s face.*) Sorry, forget I said it.

DAN: Nothing has happened to me.

LIZ: So far.

DAN: I just go about my business.

LIZ: Mr Glenn down the road got stopped the other night by

four hooded men with machine-guns. Two of them kept him up an entry while the other two took his car off to do a job. Two hours. When they came back they told him where his car was abandoned and advised him to change the number plates. Then they told him to start walking. Do you know what he said? He didn't want to leave them. He felt safer with them. He was sure if he walked away they would shoot him.

MICHAEL: What happened?

DAN: In the end they had to walk away from him.

MICHAEL: Why change the number plates?

LIZ: Because the other side would have the car identified by the number.

MICHAEL: An assassination?

LIZ: Who knows?

MICHAEL: I'll get dressed and get the papers.

DAN: While you're down there get me the *Beano*.

(MICHAEL *goes upstairs.* DAN *turns back to record.*)

LIZ: Dan, please. I want to talk to you.

DAN: There's nothing to say.

(*Enter* SMYTH *and* TULLY.)

SMYTH: Sorry, missus, it's no go. We can't fix it.

LIZ: Why not?

TULLY: We haven't the right part.

SMYTH: We'll have to come back.

LIZ: When?

SMYTH: It'll have to be next week.

LIZ: That's far too long, we can't be without heat.

SMYTH: If they hijack a few vans or the like it could be the week after.

TULLY: It's out of our control.

SMYTH: It's not our fault.

LIZ: No, I suppose not.

TULLY: We'll do our best.

SMYTH: We'll put you top of our list.

TULLY: We'll let ourselves out.

DAN: Leave the door open.

SMYTH: Are you sure, mister?

DAN: It's the way I want to live.

SMYTH: Fair enough. Do like the man says, Tully. We'll see you, Monday morning.

(SMYTH *and* TULLY *exit.*)

LIZ: What did you do? Give him the Masonic password?

DAN: I don't know. Liz, before you speak a word. Could I have some coffee?

LIZ: Oh . . . all right.

(LIZ *exits to kitchen.*

DAN *puts headphones on again.*

MICHAEL *enters dressed to go out.*)

MICHAEL: There's a naked girl upstairs. Well, not completely, but I met her coming out of the bathroom in nothing but a towel. Beautiful.

(DAN *can't hear.* MICHAEL *mimes meeting the girl and what he'd like to do to her.* DAN *takes headphones off.*)

DAN: Don't tell me, let me guess. You bugger Sphinxes.

MICHAEL: Who's the chick upstairs?

DAN: Carol. You met her last night.

MICHAEL: Did I?

DAN: When we came in.

MICHAEL: I must have been pissed.

DAN: She's a student. She was baby-sitting.

MICHAEL: Is she staying tonight?

DAN: I think she has to go home.

MICHAEL: I might make her change her mind. Don't let her leave before I get back.

(MICHAEL *exits.*)

DAN: What am I going to do? Sit on her?

(LIZ *enters.*)

LIZ: You'll have to wait for your coffee. Those workmen drank a whole pot. Dan, please turn that record off.

(DAN *stops it.*)

Your daughter told me last night I was a fucking nuisance.

DAN: Were you?

LIZ: It's not funny. She picks it up from you.

DAN: When?

LIZ: When you . . . Oh Dan, what way is this to bring up a

child?

DAN: Here? In Belfast? Now?

LIZ: Yes. Here.

DAN: I haven't a fucking clue.

LIZ: She deserves a better answer. Why don't you come home and play with her? Why are you never here?

DAN: Because.

LIZ: Because what?

DAN: Because.

LIZ: This isn't a home.

DAN: What is it then?

LIZ: It's a dirty house.

DAN: Why?

LIZ: I've decided to stop cleaning it.

DAN: What about Rosy?

LIZ: I'll clean for her.

DAN: Why not me?

LIZ: Because I'm not getting paid for the job.

DAN: Take your clothes off.

LIZ: No. You don't want me.

DAN: You only mentioned getting paid.

LIZ: I don't need you.

DAN: Fine.

LIZ: I don't need you for that. I can do that to myself. I've got my dreams as well. I can imagine some young man with muscles like a dancer who will flow all over me.

DAN: It is better than hoovering the living-room.

LIZ: I need you to come home. I need us all to sit down and eat together. I need to lie beside you and talk about nothing. Not have you come in at midnight and sit down here with the whiskey bottle. Are you afraid of us?

DAN: No.

LIZ: What's wrong with me?

DAN: Nothing.

LIZ: I could understand if you were tired of me, but what about your daughter? She's just a little child? Why don't you come home and see her?

DAN: I can't help you.

LIZ: Then I don't see any future, Dan.

DAN: She makes me want to cry.

LIZ: Why?

DAN: Because . . . because . . . she trusts me. She trusts everything. I can't bear to watch her playing. Painting something . . . she's completely absorbed . . . completely happy . . . completely trusting . . . completely unafraid . . . unaware of anything else around her. And I sit and watch her. And I don't know how to tell her that she should be afraid, that she should learn to look over her shoulder, to be suspicious of everyone, to trust is dangerous, fear is how to stay alive. She doesn't know yet that there are people who would kill her because she was born. Because she was born to us and we were born Protestant, part of a tribe. Born Catholic, it would be the same thing, people would want to kill her for it. For being born, the one thing she can't help. Although, what the hell, she can grow up to do no harm to anyone and still be marked on somebody's card. I don't know how to tell her that growing up is still worthwhile. I don't know if I believe it. I don't know how to tell her that I am helpless . . . that I feel helpless to defend her . . . and helpless to secure her future. She just laughs and puts her arms around me and hugs me and believes that when Daddy kisses it it makes it better.

LIZ: So do I, I believe that too, Dan.

DAN: It's no answer. I've got nothing in my bag.

LIZ: Dan . . .

DAN: Maybe you'd be better with somebody else. Leave me alone, Liz.

(LIZ *is hurt by this. Hesitates, then goes into kitchen.* DAN *puts on headphones and starts record. Changes his mind, pulls plug out so music fills room.*

CAROL *enters from upstairs. Nineteen, attractive, still some of the awkwardness of adolescence.*)

DAN: Charlie Parker was called Yardbird, Bird for short. He was my boyhood hero. He played the alto saxophone. In the bebop revolution. He died when he was thirty-four. He was a drug addict. When he died a doctor was called who didn't know him. He wrote on the death certificate—a male negro, aged about sixty years. The day after there appeared scrawled on the walls all over Harlem, two words—BIRD LIVES.

CAROL: When did he die?

DAN: 1955.

CAROL: I wasn't born then. I'd rather have Andy Williams.

(CAROL *goes into the kitchen.* DAN *picks up warm underpants, loosens gown ready to put them on.*

MICHAEL, *a pile of papers under his arm, bursts in. Followed by* BOYD, *a lawyer, former politician, and long-time friend of* DAN *and* MICHAEL.)

MICHAEL: Dan, did you know about this?

DAN: About what?

MICHAEL: Tell him, Boyd, tell him what you just told me.

BOYD: How are you, Dan?

DAN: Surviving.

BOYD: Fancy coming out for a drink?

DAN: It's a bit early.

MICHAEL: I don't understand it. I really don't understand it. I don't understand your reason.

BOYD: Reason has nothing to do with it.

DAN: Do you need a drink?

BOYD: I wouldn't mind.

DAN: Help yourself.

(BOYD *pours himself a whiskey.*)

Michael?

MICHAEL: No thanks. What has happened to the two of you?

DAN: What has happened? (*Stops record.*)

BOYD: Nothing much.

MICHAEL: Nothing! You've just told me that you've given up, had to give up. That you've been driven out of politics.

BOYD: I haven't much choice.

MICHAEL: But, if someone like you gives up . . . I mean, you're both socialists. . . .

BOYD: Dan has left the Party.

MICHAEL: What are you now?

DAN: Cold. Boyd, would you keep an eye on the kitchen while I get dressed, the baby-sitter is in there?

BOYD: Do I have to watch you?

DAN: Suit yourself.

(DAN *strips off completely, ready to put his clothes on.*)

MICHAEL: I don't understand.

BOYD: Look at him.

MICHAEL: Why?

BOYD: Look.

(*All look at naked* DAN.)

If we were evolving properly, he would be bullet-proof. But we're not. If you want evidence that we don't adapt to our environment and that evolution is all a cruel accident, look at him. It's just not up to the job. Look at the skin. What a pathetic envelope.

DAN: It is waterproof.

BOYD: You're not likely to get licked to death.

DAN: True. (*Goes on dressing.*)

BOYD: What a piece of work. Hair pulls out. One speck in your eye is enough. Did you ever get hit on the nose? Incapacitates you. Ears can be bitten off. Neck, shoulders, arms, spine, all dislocate with a single twist. Would you call those ribs a decent battlement? Liver and kidneys exposed to one sharp dig. And as for his balls, one good squeeze and he'd sing a high C that would crack glasses. Legs can't outrun a bullet.

MICHAEL: We have a brain. We can think.

BOYD: That's the easiest of all. One injection. Or put the hood over my head, play the noise in my ears, stand me in a corner for three days, and I'll break myself with my ability to think.

(DAN *finishes dressing, switches off electric fire.*)

Or just frighten me enough, or fill my head with hate from the moment I can stand.

MICHAEL: You make a mistake. You talk as if our environment was natural. And that we no longer fit it. We are natural. It is unnatural.

BOYD: We made it. People made it. It wasn't sun-spots, God or the Devil.

DAN: Why are you giving up?
BOYD: I got another threat this morning.
MICHAEL: A threat on your life?
BOYD: Yes.
MICHAEL: Christ. That's different. You didn't tell me that. Who from?
BOYD: They're anonymous phone calls. I know it's very stupid of me, and probably very weak of me, but I am absolutely terrified.
DAN: That's not stupid.
BOYD: You know as well as I do that threatening people is normal political action here. It was bound to happen. It's just that they're so persistent.
MICHAEL: Haven't you told the police?
BOYD: A Special Branch man came round. He was very friendly. He looked like a family butcher, you know, face like a slab of his own meat. Basically, he said, if I could give them any real evidence of who was making the calls, they'd be able to do something about it.
MICHAEL: How can you prove that?
BOYD: I can't. It's different voices.
DAN: It could be anybody. Heard you on television and didn't fancy what you said. UDA, IRA, UVF, UFF, or some other F we haven't heard of.
MICHAEL: But they've given you protection?
BOYD: If they tried to protect everybody who was threatened they'd need another army.
MICHAEL: But you are a politician.
BOYD: I was, Michael, I was. I lost the last two elections to a man who believes that Socialists have cloven feet and a tail and that God came from Ballymena.
MICHAEL: So what did they do?
BOYD: He told me not to stand at any lighted windows. I've told others to stand firm, but it's different when it happens to you. I don't know what to do.
DAN: You didn't dream about a black cat last night?
BOYD: No.
MICHAEL: You must get a gun.

BOYD: What?

MICHAEL: Get a gun.

BOYD: You're not serious?

MICHAEL: You have to protect yourself.

BOYD: Is that . . . is that your solution?

MICHAEL: I'm being practical. Dan, don't you think he should get a gun?

DAN: Could you shoot somebody?

MICHAEL: I . . . I don't know.

DAN: Have you ever handled a gun?

MICHAEL: No. But he has the right to defend himself.

BOYD: I'd be more liable to shoot myself.

DAN: I was taught to kill at my grammar school, my Protestant grammar school. It was part of our leisure activities. In the Army Cadet Force. It wasn't exactly compulsory but the Headmaster was also the head officer and the advantages of joining were pretty firmly put to you. I had a uniform, British. We were attached to a real regiment, we had Regular Army instructors. I learned the principles of command, communications and guerilla warfare. I rose to the rank of sergeant. I could strip and assemble a Bren gun in under sixty seconds, and with a rifle I could put five bullets in a space an inch across at twenty-five yards. I have a badge to prove it. It was called an Empire Marksman badge. My finest moment came when, one Speech Day, I led a guard of honour for his colonial eminence, the British Governor of Northern Ireland. I walked beside him as he inspected our brave troop. In the photographs I have the face of a trapped rat and he has the face of an old drunk. I'd be hard put now to tell you the causes of the First World War but I still get excited by a gun in my hand. I won't touch one now.

MICHAEL: But he must be protected.

BOYD: If they ever get me, it will be sometime, maybe in the morning when I'm making breakfast, when I won't even see them.

MICHAEL: Is there no hope for this place? Is that what you're saying? I don't believe it, I can't believe it. You can't give up hope, you can't give up the struggle. The only way forward here is to break out of the old mindless, useless sectarian conflict, into the real struggle, between exploiter and exploited, the conflict of right and left; non-violent, democratic, but militant struggle. And for that you need leadership.

BOYD: I have a wife and children.

DAN: What does Rachel say?

BOYD: Would you come round and talk to her?

DAN: Yes.

BOYD: She's been . . . terrific . . . but every time the phone rings we're leaping there to get ahead of the kids, in case. And sometimes she's been alone in the house. . . .

MICHAEL: What sort of things do they say?

BOYD: They're quite polite about it. And that's worse, because then your imagination gets to work. I mean, what if I'm out with one of the kids and I'm machine-gunned and the child has to watch me bleeding to death in front of her. . . . Michael, I'm just a man.

DAN: What do you want me to say to Rachel?

BOYD: She's just had too much this morning. She's taken a pill, she's just sitting. She wants us to pack up and leave Ulster. Can you explain to her that I can't do that? I just can't do that.

MICHAEL: What will you do?

BOYD: Not stand at any lighted windows.

DAN: I'll come with you now.

(*There is a knock on the living-room door.*)

BOYD: Are you expecting anybody?

DAN: No. Did anybody follow you?

BOYD: I don't know.

MICHAEL: This is broad daylight.

(LIZ *enters from kitchen.*)

LIZ: Is nobody going to answer that?

DAN: Go back in the kitchen.

LIZ: Why?

(*Living-room door opens.* BERTHA *comes in. Large, about forty, next-door neighbour.*)

BERTHA: (*Calls*) Hellooo. (*Sees them.*) What's up? What are you all looking at? Have I forgotten to put on my skirt?

DAN: Why did you knock?

BERTHA: Out of politeness. I didn't want to just barge in. I didn't know all you lot were here. I just came round for a cup of coffee with Liz.

DAN: This is Bertha, our next-door neighbour. You know Boyd.

BERTHA: Hello.

DAN: This is Michael, a friend of ours from a long time ago. He lives in London now, he's a lecturer.

BERTHA: Hello.

MICHAEL: Bertha.

BERTHA: If it's not convenient, I'll go out again.

DAN: We're going out.

LIZ: Where to?

DAN: Round to Boyd's house for a while. We'll be back.

BOYD: Bye, Liz.

LIZ: I didn't even get the chance to say hello.

MICHAEL: (*To* BERTHA) Nice to meet you.

BERTHA: (*Coyly*) Nice to meet you.

(MICHAEL *and* BOYD *go out.*)

LIZ: Well, will you be back for lunch or will you go straight to the pub?

DAN: Lunch.

LIZ: What will I make? Something I can throw away or something we can eat cold tomorrow?

DAN: Suit yourself.

LIZ: What's going on? What are you going round there for?

DAN: There's something wrong with his car, that's all.

BERTHA: Bring that nice Michael back to us in one piece.

DAN: He wouldn't be fit for you, Bertha.

BERTHA: That's the trouble with all you men these days.

(DAN *exits.* BERTHA *flops in a chair.*)

LIZ: What's up?

BERTHA: That husband of mine. I wanted him to take the kids to their Granny's for the afternoon and then come back and he and I would have a bit of peace together, you know. I even made sure he saw me put on the black stockings and the suspender belt. And what does he say?—Agh, I think I'll just stay over there, there's a match on and she has a colour telly.

LIZ: Get him to buy you one.

BERTHA: He'd still escape.

LIZ: (*Calls into the kitchen*) Carol, would you put the coffee pot on again?

BERTHA: Carol?

LIZ: You know, she baby-sits for us sometimes. She stayed last night.

BERTHA: Who's that nice Michael? I could fancy him.

LIZ: I knew him at university.

BERTHA: Married?

LIZ: Yes.

BERTHA: Just over here on a wee break?

LIZ: I asked him to come.

BERTHA: Oh?

LIZ: It's not what you think.

BERTHA: I'm not thinking anything. All the decent men go away. I was looking at a photograph of myself the other day. I was beautiful. You wouldn't think it, but I was. And innocent. I was eighteen when I married Frank and I knew nothing, literally nothing. It's as well I didn't know what was going to happen to me or I'd have cut my throat.

(*Enter* CAROL *with tray and coffee for two.*)

CAROL: I've made your coffee.

LIZ: I just meant put the pot on I would have done the rest, but thank you.

BERTHA: Hello.

CAROL: Hello.

LIZ: Aren't you having any?

CAROL: No, I'll go upstairs and finish dressing. Will I take this? (*Indicates* DAN'*s dressing-gown on couch.*)

LIZ: Please.

(CAROL *exits,* LIZ *pours coffee.*)

BERTHA: God, it would make you jealous.

LIZ: Her?

BERTHA: No, I don't envy any child growing up now. I'm sure

she's not as innocent as I was.

LIZ: In some ways she is. As innocent as Rosy.

BERTHA: I wonder they don't hate us for the mess we've left them. No, I meant your house.

LIZ: Why?

BERTHA: It represents peace to me. Civilized. Somewhere to escape. Away from Frank's oul mother. That woman. I'm going to tell you something. Do you know the only thing that makes her perk up any more? Whips. I was watching her the other night and just realized it. She goes on about what she would do. The ones she wouldn't hang she would flog and love every minute of it. A twelve-year-old goes out and throws a brick in a riot, imitating his elders, she'd give him the birch. If he's a Catholic. If he's a Protestant she'd give him a medal. And my children have to listen to that. This house is an oasis.

LIZ: It doesn't seem like that to me. We're pretending. We couldn't defend this because we don't know what we have to defend. Dan wouldn't defend it.

BERTHA: Any man would defend his own home. Even Frank.

LIZ: Dan wants to live the way we always lived, the way we lived before. But we can't.

BERTHA: I want to live now.

(BERTHA *goes round checking doors and closing them.*)

Is that wee girl going to come back?

LIZ: I wouldn't think for a while. Why?

BERTHA: I don't want to be talking about my sex life in front of her. You don't mind though, do you? I have to talk to somebody.

LIZ: I don't mind.

BERTHA: It's just that there's not much of it so I like to stretch it out by talking about it. You know I have this bad back. Well, I thought I'd slipped a disc.

(*Hall door opens,* CAROL *enters.*)

Lovely day today, isn't it?

LIZ: What is it, Carol?

CAROL: Will you remember my money? In case you're going out.

LIZ: I'll be here.

CAROL: It's just I bought these jeans in a sale and then I saw this top and I couldn't resist it so I spent all my money, my train fare home.

LIZ: I'll pay you for next week-end as well if you like.

CAROL: I can't stay next week-end.

LIZ: (*Disappointed*) Oh.

CAROL: You see, I wouldn't get any money.

LIZ: What?

CAROL: Daddy gives me my allowance every week so I can't afford not to go home.

BERTHA: Do you not have a bank account, dear?

CAROL: Daddy pays the hostel and all by cheque.

BERTHA: You're old enough to vote.

CAROL: I think I can make a sensible judgement.

BERTHA: Can big Daddy?

CAROL: Mrs Poots . . .

LIZ: Liz, you must call me Liz.

CAROL: Liz . . . could you or Mr Poots give me a lift to the station later?

LIZ: Of course.

CAROL: (*Stopping at door*) Oh, and can I borrow a book?

LIZ: Of course.

BERTHA: What's the book?

CAROL: 'Fear of Flying'.

(CAROL *exits.*)

BERTHA: Well.

LIZ: You're safe now. Who was the man?

BERTHA: He works where a friend of mine works. I met him a few times, lunch and that. Married, of course, but youngish, and fit, a very good body. I like that. Dead stupid, but you can't be too fussy. So we arranged it for his afternoon off. His wife works. Well, first of all, I had to follow so many instructions getting there so the neighbours wouldn't see me, and he has the curtains drawn. He gives me a drink and already he's looking at his watch. I hardly have time for a sip when he says, 'Let's go upstairs.' No clean sheets, but a towel. The situations I get into. He strips off. And, right enough, he has this very pretty penis. Well, when I say pretty, I don't know, I haven't seen that many and none of them were in beauty competitions, but he has . . . a big cock. I start to undress and then he takes over, very slow. He has this mood music on and it's getting me going. Well, I'm beginning to wonder is all this just another gentlemen's excuse me, but, at last, we're on the bed and he's all there, you know. Well. He starts. Now, Liz, I know people do these things and I didn't want to show my ignorance, I was willing, but I was practically on top of the wardrobe. Back, front and sideways, never stopped. Two minutes this way, I'm only getting used to it, and then all change. I thought I won't get out of here without a slipped disc, they'll have to take me in an ambulance. And not one word of conversation, except, every position, he says, 'How does that grab you?' Would you credit that? 'How does that grab you?' If I came once, I came twenty times, and when I come an express train wouldn't be in it. He practically gagged me. And do you know this? I was bored, bored out of my mind. All I wanted was a simple bit of pleasure. I don't know how his poor wife stands it.

LIZ: He never does those things with his wife.

BERTHA: You don't think so?

LIZ: I bet he doesn't even dare suggest it. I bet you he had never done any of those before.

BERTHA: Well, he certainly knew his way.

LIZ: He read about them and thought everybody else was having a good time except him.

BERTHA: He's done them all now. I hope he didn't have the impression I was the sort would know all those things.

LIZ: He never thought about you.

BERTHA: That's a cruel thing to say.

LIZ: I mean as a person. You were his fantasy.

BERTHA: How does that grab you? Liz, I only have the one life, and not much left of it at that. Why do we live like this?

LIZ: I wish I knew.

BERTHA: I asked my Frank.

LIZ: What did he say?

BERTHA: He said if I didn't stop asking him stupid questions he'd go home to his mother. (*Pause*) Would you ever be unfaithful to Dan?

LIZ: I don't know what that means. He doesn't own me. He didn't buy me in a shop. I don't belong to him. I've no real objection. I just couldn't stand the boredom.

BERTHA: Frank would kill me if he knew. He's not a bad man. He's . . . ohhh . . . I wish I'd never looked at that photograph of myself. I think I'll burn it.

LIZ: No. No.

(*Enter* MICHAEL.)

MICHAEL: Sorry . . . I thought you'd be alone, Liz . . . I mean . . .

BERTHA: It's all right. I'm just going.

LIZ: You don't have to.

BERTHA: I've the washing to do. You be good to her, Michael.

MICHAEL: What?

BERTHA: I'll go out the back way.

(BERTHA *and* LIZ *move to back.* LIZ *slides glass door open.*)

LIZ: Go this way. It's as easy as going out the kitchen.

BERTHA: OK.

LIZ: Leave the back gate.

BERTHA: We just have to keep going, don't we? As if life was normal. Isn't that what we're all so proud of? Bye.

(BERTHA *goes out.* LIZ *closes glass door.* MICHAEL *comes to her, puts his arms round her, kisses her, she responds briefly, but when he tries to prolong it she slips away.*)

MICHAEL: How are you?

LIZ: All right.

MICHAEL: I'm here.

LIZ: Yes.

MICHAEL: Well?

LIZ: It's good to see you.

MICHAEL: I got such a shock when I met you last night.

LIZ: Why?

MICHAEL: I looked at an old photograph of you, before I came over. . . .

LIZ: I'm different now.

MICHAEL: No. That's the point. You are just the same. Just as I remember you.

LIZ: I'm not.

MICHAEL: You are. I was such a fool.

LIZ: We can't go back.

MICHAEL: I came as soon as I got your letter.

LIZ: Oh that?

MICHAEL: Yes.

LIZ: I forget what I said.

MICHAEL: You asked me to come.

LIZ: Well . . . I just needed someone to write to at the time.

MICHAEL: But you thought of me.

LIZ: Yes.

MICHAEL: So you needed me.

LIZ: I didn't really expect you to come.

MICHAEL: You knew I would.

LIZ: It was an impulse.

MICHAEL: You didn't tell me in the letter what happened.

LIZ: Let's not talk about it.

MICHAEL: Tell me. I would do anything for you.

LIZ: I know. I suppose I know that.

MICHAEL: (*Moving closer to her*) I would.

LIZ: Would you like some coffee?

MICHAEL: Was it something Dan did?

LIZ: It's past.

MICHAEL: I read your letter.

LIZ: I don't know what's the matter with him.

MICHAEL: Tell me about it.

LIZ: He attacked me. He put me out of the house. Both of us. Rosy and me.

MICHAEL: When was this?

LIZ: The middle of the night.

MICHAEL: Dan did?

LIZ: I don't know what has happened. Inside him. It's not like the old days. People don't go out. You can't just go and sit in a pub. He has fewer and fewer real friends. We can't go out together, we can't get baby-sitters very often. People just stay at home and survive. He came home one night, he wasn't sober. That's been happening more and more. I don't nag at him, at least I don't think I do, I try not to. But I must have said something, I don't know what I said. We were in the kitchen. Whatever I said, something just . . . it just snapped in him.

MICHAEL: And what happened?

LIZ: He picked up the kitchen knife and went for me. He isn't violent, Michael, he never was, he never hit me, it's not in him. He was like a different person, waving the knife and shouting, just to stop, stop being, stop being around him. I asked him to put the knife down. Eventually he did. But he was still raving. Then he went to hit me and I stood there. I must have been shouting too, although I was trying to calm him. It wakened Rosy and she came down in her night-gown. She was crying. It made him worse. She was dragging at his legs, trying to pull him away from me, stop him hitting me. He just wanted rid of us. I got hold of Rosy. I didn't care then what he did to me as long as he didn't hurt her. She'd never seen her Daddy like this. He told me to take her and get out. I was in my dressing-gown, but I was so afraid of him by then that I just grabbed up a rug and wrapped her in it and ran into the street. He locked the door on us. He never locks the door. I lock the door.

MICHAEL: What did you do?

LIZ: Waited. He put all the lights out. It was too cold and Rosy was too upset, I couldn't wait long, so I went round to Boyd's. Boyd came round here in the morning and Dan behaved as if nothing had happened, asked where we were and all, and Boyd came and brought us round. I made the breakfast, he went to work, Rosy went to school.

MICHAEL: Have you talked about it?

LIZ: I'm not even sure he knows what happened.

MICHAEL: He must.

LIZ: We just go on. Except he drinks more. And now he won't come home while Rosy is up, he hardly sees her.

MICHAEL: How is she?

LIZ: She's sort of forgotten.

MICHAEL: Has it happened again?

LIZ: No. I try and make a home for him. I try to be

interesting. I have my job, my own car, he's free. But he can't talk to me. What am I going to do?

MICHAEL: You're going to come away with me.

LIZ: What?

MICHAEL: You can't stay. You don't want to stay. That's what you said in your letter.

LIZ: I didn't say that.

MICHAEL: That's what you meant. And it's what I want.

LIZ: But you . . .

MICHAEL: I want to take you away. To take you and Rosy away from here. I came here to do that. To save you.

LIZ: But you didn't know all this.

MICHAEL: I know how I feel about you. How I have always felt about you. Liz, the greatest mistake of my life was when I left you.

LIZ: I left you.

MICHAEL: When I got your letter it made me . . . it was like seeing light at the end of a tunnel. Come with me. If not for my sake, for the sake of Rosy.

LIZ: But you are married.

MICHAEL: We separated. She left me. It was either her or me. We would have destroyed each other. We had no children. I can see the same thing here. Don't destroy yourselves. Let me save you. This is no place to bring up a child. Liz. . . . (*Takes* LIZ *in his arms.*) Liz, I'm more in love with you than ever I was. I need you both. Come with me.

LIZ: My husband is here.

MICHAEL: What have you left between you? Except fighting. Let me take care of you.

(*Very close. For a moment* LIZ *would be content just to give in and be held but she pulls away.*)

LIZ: You make it sound as if it was all Dan's fault. Or as if I have no will of my own. I have. I'm to blame here too. I have a responsibility here. We made this together.

MICHAEL: And it is over.

LIZ: It is not over just because it seems hopeless now. By God, we are not always going to live like this. No, Michael, no, no, no, no, no.

MICHAEL: But what about me?

LIZ: I didn't marry you.

MICHAEL: But . . . I'm right . . . I know I'm right. Your future is with me.

LIZ: I have to go now. I have to collect Rosy from her class. I'm taking her to her grandmother. I may stay there all afternoon.

MICHAEL: Don't go.

LIZ: Tell Dan where I am.

MICHAEL: Don't go.

(LIZ *grabs up her coat and bag.*)

LIZ: I must.

(LIZ *runs out, to front.*)

MICHAEL: It isn't fair.

(MICHAEL *is very upset, even a bit unbalanced. It is the beginning of an inner hysteria which will grow. He makes a big effort to calm himself.* CAROL *enters urgently from upstairs.*)

CAROL: Was that Mrs Poots driving away?

MICHAEL: Yes, it was.

CAROL: Did she leave any money for me?

MICHAEL: I don't think so.

CAROL: Is there nobody here?

MICHAEL: I'm here.

CAROL: Oh shit. How am I going to get home? (*Takes out fags.*)

MICHAEL: Do you have to?

CAROL: Daddy would kill me if I didn't. I need the money for the train fare. Do you smoke?

MICHAEL: No. What does Daddy do?

CAROL: He's a teacher. (*Lights up.*) Are you a teacher?

MICHAEL: No. I'm a lecturer. And I think I'm going mad.

CAROL: Aren't we all? I don't want to go home. It's just like going to the toilet.

MICHAEL: What?

CAROL: Doing your duty. When my brother and I were younger we had to go at a certain time every day to do, you know, number two. My father had a list and gave us all a time. Mine was seven-thirty during term time and ten o'clock in the holidays. Daddy would look at his watch and compare it with the clock and then say, 'Up you go,' and you'd have to go and sit there, whether you wanted to do anything or not. And you weren't allowed to take anything to read. He was always moving about outside, up and down the stairs. And when your time was up he'd come knocking on the door and he always asked 'Did you do your duty?' Do you wonder I like this house? I never want to leave it when I'm here.

MICHAEL: I need a drink. Do you want one?

CAROL: I shouldn't—is there any vodka?

MICHAEL: Doesn't smell the breath, eh? (*Heads for drinks.*)

CAROL: So they say. Thanks.

(CAROL *flops in a chair, puffs her cigarette, trying to look as sophisticated as possible in her new gear.*)

MICHAEL: I like the gear.

CAROL: Thanks.

MICHAEL: (*Back to her*) Do you always wear a bra?

CAROL: (*A little unnerved*) Yes.

MICHAEL: Otherwise Daddy would kill you.

CAROL: He just . . . likes discipline.

MICHAEL: I'll bet.

CAROL: I really envy Rosy, I wish I was her. Only my age.

MICHAEL: (*Coming back with drinks*) What do you want to do when you leave . . . where is it?

CAROL: Teacher training college.

MICHAEL: Just like Daddy.

CAROL: I didn't choose it. I want to get away . . . anywhere. You come from London, don't you?

MICHAEL: Yes.

CAROL: What do they think of us over there?

MICHAEL: They want to forget they ever had an Empire but the like of your Daddy will keep reminding them. Away back at the beginning of these troubles I saw a photograph in the paper of a bunch of women demonstrating outside an Army Post. One of them carried a placard which read 'Poisoned Dwarfs Go Home'. I would say the feeling is mutual.

CAROL: Some of us are still normal.

MICHAEL: Then isn't your responsibility here?

CAROL: I want a normal life, I want children of my own. I have to get away. But what chance have I got? Are you married?

MICHAEL: No. (*Fetches bottle, tops himself up.*) No, I'm not, I never have been married. I feel as if my life has never started. I don't seem to have what other people do.

CAROL: But you live in London.

MICHAEL: You see . . . I understand . . . I understand it all perfectly . . . but I can't do anything about it. I mean, I must, I can, I must, it is a responsibility. I must be going mad. . . . I can see . . . everything . . . perfectly clearly. Perfectly, absolutely, clearly. But who will take care of us?

CAROL: God will. Didn't you know that? After we're dead of course.

MICHAEL: Somebody must help you. Another drink?

CAROL: I should go home.

MICHAEL: I'll give you the money.

CAROL: Just one. (MICHAEL *fills her glass.*) You're making me nervous. I've never met anyone like you before.

MICHAEL: I'm not special. Well . . . I suppose. . . . Do you have a boyfriend?

CAROL: No. The boys here are all straight off the farm. They think we're cows.

MICHAEL: Do you know the trouble with fucking cows?

CAROL: No. What?

MICHAEL: You have to keep running round the front to kiss them. (CAROL *breaks up in laughter.*)

CAROL: This vodka's going to my head.

MICHAEL: And mine.

CAROL: What's it really like in London?

MICHAEL: Do you want to go there? I'll take you.

CAROL: For a week-end?

MICHAEL: For as long as you want. I would take care of you. You can be free.

CAROL: (*Getting up, a pause*) Would I have to sleep with you?

MICHAEL: No.

CAROL: Do you want to sleep with me now?

MICHAEL: Daddy would kill you.

CAROL: No, I'll kill Daddy. (*Hands him her glass.*) My room's at the top of the house. (*Pauses at door as she goes.*) In case anyone would come in.

(CAROL *goes out.*)

MICHAEL: What the hell have I done?

(DAN *enters through the glass doors at the back.*)

DAN: I thought you were coming back to Boyd's.

MICHAEL: What? I was. I am. I am coming now.

DAN: It won't do any good.

MICHAEL: Let's go out for a drink.

DAN: No. Who's been drinking vodka? Probably big Bertha. Watch out for her. Big Bertha would bounce you round the bed like a boomerang.

(DAN *goes to the stereo.*)

MICHAEL: Liz has taken Rosy to her grandmother's. She said she might be late. I was talking to her.

DAN: Were you?

MICHAEL: Yes. She was telling me about things.

(DAN *puts on headphones, ready to start record.*)

Do you know what you're doing to her? What's got into you?

DAN: Eh?

MICHAEL: What the hell's got into you?

DAN: (*Taking headphones off*) What?

MICHAEL: What's got into you?

DAN: What's got into you?

MICHAEL: Nothing.

DAN: Then nothing's got into me. (*Puts headphones on.*)

MICHAEL: If you don't care about your wife, at least . . . at least care about your child. It is the greatest despair in my life that I have no children. I don't know . . . I don't know what the hell I'm living for. I have to live for something or someone, I can't just live for myself. You can't either.

DAN: (*Slips headphones down round his neck*) You make it sound as if I have a choice. I have lived all my life in an Old Testament farce. I used to lie on the floor of my cousin's front room with my ear pressed to an old gramophone to hear the sounds of the twentieth century, the sounds of 52nd Street in the Big Apple. Charlie Parker blew in my ear, saying survival is not enough. He didn't join and he wasn't going to rebel because he couldn't join, he simply found the terms of membership unacceptable. So do I. He pulled down his shades and said, don't fool yourself, there is no shining light, but, while I can, I will perform an impossible feat for you, I will shine. But he was dead at thirty-four. I got an old clarinet and then a sax. It wasn't approved of, it wasn't respectable, you couldn't take an exam in bebop, and they don't play the saxophone in Orange bands. So I told lies to get out and play with a pre-electric six-piece called The Rhythm Kings. Terrible stuff. The singer wore a cowboy suit and yodelled. They loved him. But for the first hour of the dance when nobody was in I could play the solos, copied off the record. I never had the talent, but, by Jesus, I had the contempt. I was doing more than surviving. But when I was eighteen and leaving school my father brought me into the front room and he said, you're going to be a teacher. I said no. I thought he was going to hit me, which was his solution to everything. I was ready for that. Instead he did something so unexpected that it really floored me. He asked me what I wanted to do. I didn't know. A week later I was doing pharmacy. I was back to surviving. And now I've had eight years of troubles. It's the only life I have, I'll never get to live it again in peace and freedom having fun while my family grows. It's gone. I'm on the road and it's too late to stop now, no crossroads left, no end in sight, a blind, black cat for company. I still find the terms unacceptable. In the beginning all I wanted was get into some sweet cunt, then I discovered love, and I wish to die without an ounce of spunk left in me. That's my order of things. But when people get the order wrong then they fall in love with death and worship statues of men in their last agony, or fall in love with substitute pricks and start shoving guns up cunts. Murder is always impotence. Of the killer and the killed. A perversion of the spirit. And for the last six months my cock has not raised its head. Now either my time has come or it is just afraid of getting its knob shot off. I am surviving. And I am cold.

MICHAEL: I think I'll go upstairs for a while. Unpack. . . .

DAN: Take all the time you want.

(DAN *turns to stereo as* MICHAEL *goes out. Starts record, it fills the room.*)

'Lover Man', written by Ramirez, Davis and Sherman. Charlie Parker, alto; Howard McGhee, trumpet; Jimmy Bunn, piano; Roy Porter, drums; and Dingbod Kesterson, bass. Whatever happened to old Dingbod?

(*A tall man,* MAC, *appears beyond the glass doors. He wears army surplus jacket and jeans. One hand behind his back. Looks round room, then uses his free hand to pull a balaclava hood over his head. It has space cut out for eyes and mouth. Brings the other hand from behind his back holding a machine-gun. He slides the door back and steps in followed by a boy,* BILLY. MAGOO *enters from the kitchen, followed by* SHORTY, *who has a tool-bag, and swiftly checks the doors. At this* DAN *turns and sees the line of four hooded figures.* MAC *points the gun at* DAN.)

MAC: Rest easy, friend.

CURTAIN

ACT TWO

The act begins where Act One stopped with no break of stage time. DAN *confronts the hooded men. The track of the record starts.* MAC *gestures with the gun.* MAGOO *steps forward, turns it off.*

MAGOO: What kind of rotten oul music is that?
MAC: Is that your car outside?
DAN: Why?
MAC: There's nothing to worry about, friend. We just want to borrow your car.
DAN: Why?
MAC: What you don't know won't hurt you. Isn't that a fact? Give us the keys.
DAN: Take them.
MAC: Be sensible, friend.
DAN: Why?
MAC: Anybody else in the house?
DAN: No. They're by the records.
MAC: Get them.
(DAN *doesn't move.* MAC *gestures to* MAGOO.)
You.
MAGOO: Where are they? I don't see them.
MAC: Over there.
MAGOO: Where?
MAC: Under your nose.
MAGOO: Hang on.
(MAGOO *produces round, thick-lensed National Health spectacles, has trouble putting them over his hood. Peers around.*)
Oh, right, I see them now.
(MAGOO *hands the keys to* MAC.)

MAC: What's your name, friend?

DAN: Why?

MAC: There's nothing to worry about. Tell us your name.

DAN: Poots.

MAC: What sort of a name is that?

SHORTY: It's a Protestant name.

(*They all relax a little.*)

MAC: We have a job to do. All you have to do is co-operate. We just want to borrow your car for a while. You'll have it back.

DAN: Take it.

MAC: Good. I like it friendly. (*To* SHORTY.) Get outside and start the car. (*Hands over keys.*) And remember to take your hood off first. Have you got the tool-bag?

SHORTY: Here.

MAC: Right. (*Puts machine-gun in it.*) If anyone's looking let them see the bag.

SHORTY: Right.

(*Exit* SHORTY.)

MAC: New car?

DAN: Yes.

MAC: (*Looking around*) You've got all your orders here. Just stay on our side.

DAN: I'm. . . .

MAC: What?

DAN: I'm on my own.

MAC: So you are, friend. Right, let's go.

(MAC *moves to door.* BILLY *goes ahead of him.*)

Not you.

BILLY: Why not? Why not? You're not leaving me behind again? Why pick on me? It's my turn.

MAC: You do what I tell you, when I tell you. Right?

BILLY: It's not fair.

MAC: Your turn'll come.

BILLY: When?

MAC: When I say. (*To* MAGOO.) You know what to do?

MAGOO: Yes. Yes, sir.

MAC: I'll see the both of you later.

DAN: Are you leaving me with these two?
MAC: I have to, friend.
DAN: Take the car.
MAC: You would pick up the phone.
DAN: Then tie me up.
MAC: That'll happen anyway. Just relax. I told you, nobody will hurt you.
DAN: Could I. . . .
MAC: What?
DAN: Could I have a pee?
MAC: It happens to everybody to feel like that. You'll forget about it in a minute. Relax. (*To* MAGOO.) Ready?
MAGOO: Yes, sir.
MAC: Do the job right.

(MAC *exits.*

MAGOO *produces a knife.*)

MAGOO: Turn round. I can see well enough to use this, it's close. I'm all right when it's close. Turn round.

(DAN *turns his back to* MAGOO *and* BILLY. *Now facing front.* BILLY *comes behind* DAN *and puts a blindfold on.*)

DAN: Do I have to be blind?
BILLY: (*Shoves him*) Shut your beak, you.
MAGOO: That's a gorgeous fucking way to talk, that is. Where's your manners?
BILLY: Wha'?
MAGOO: You forget what we're doing, we're doing for the like of this gentleman here, to protect him and his future. Away and get a straight chair.
BILLY: Why does he always leave me behind with you?
MAGOO: Because you never do what you're told. Get the chair.

(BILLY *goes to kitchen.*)

Stay still, mister. These young ones now have no manners at all. I don't know what the country's coming to. Have you any children yourself?

DAN: A daughter.
MAGOO: Aye, well, the sooner this is over the better, eh?

(BILLY, *with hood off, comes back with kitchen chair. Places it behind* DAN.)

Right. Sit down there. Tie him up there, Billy. Hurry up. (DAN *pushed down into chair and* BILLY, *producing a thin rope, ties him up.* MAGOO *meanwhile takes off his glasses, then his hood, then replaces glasses.* BILLY *stops.*)

BILLY: Hey.

MAGOO: Wha'?

BILLY: You called me Billy.

MAGOO: Wha'?

BILLY: (*Pointing at* DAN, *shaking his head*) That's not my name.

MAGOO: Oh. Oh yes. Sorry, sorry about that . . . Charlie. I thought you were somebody else.

BILLY: Just watch it. (*Back to tying.*)

MAGOO: Tie them tight. Charlie.

(BILLY *secures the knots. They stand back to admire the work. The phone rings.*)

BILLY: Jesus, Magoo, what'll we do?

MAGOO: I'm not Magoo.

BILLY: The phone's ringing.

MAGOO: I see it is.

BILLY: You're in charge, what'll we do?

MAGOO: We do nothing.

(*The phone goes on ringing. They can't stand it.*)

DAN: I'd better answer it.

MAGOO: You will not, mister.

DAN: People know I'm here.

MAGOO: You went out. You went out in your car.

DAN: (*Raises his head, listening for sound upstairs*) You better let me answer it.

MAGOO: No.

BILLY: Let him. We can tell him what to say.

MAGOO: Why won't it stop?

BILLY: Do something, Magoo.

MAGOO: I'm not Magoo.

BILLY: What'll I call you?

MAGOO: Call me Lieutenant.

BILLY: You're as much a Lieutenant as my arse.

MAGOO: I'm in charge.

(*They wait. Phone still rings.*)

BILLY: For fuck's sake.

MAGOO: Watch your language. (*Pause.*) Charlie.

BILLY: I tell you what'll stop it. I'll lift it off.

MAGOO: It'll also tell them somebody is here.

BILLY: I won't speak into it.

MAGOO: Oh my God, just keep away from it.

DAN: Let me answer it.

BILLY: We'll cut the wires.

MAGOO: Wha'?

BILLY: I saw it in a film once. Give us your knife.

(*The phone stops.*)

It's stopped. Will I still cut the wires?

MAGOO: We'll just follow our orders.

DAN: What are they?

MAGOO: None of your business. Ah . . . Jimmy . . . give us a fag. I need one after that. Ask your man does he want one.

BILLY: Want a fag?

DAN: Please.

(BILLY *searches in* DAN'*s pockets.*)

MAGOO: Don't be taking his, we're not thieves. Give him one of your own.

BILLY: Do you smoke Woodbines?

DAN: I'd rather have one of mine. Help yourselves.

BILLY: Right.

(BILLY *lights up* DAN'*s king size and puts one between* DAN'*s lips. Wanders round room.*)

MAGOO: Oh, that's better. You always wonder how you'll act in an emergency.

BILLY: Let's have a drink.

MAGOO: You're too young.

BILLY: I can drink more nor you anyday. Here.

(BILLY *drinks from whiskey bottle, gives it to* MAGOO *who drinks.*)

DAN: What age are you, Billy?

(BILLY *thumps him in the back.*)

BILLY: Charlie. No. My name is Charles. You hear nobody say Charlie Bronson. It's Charles. I'm sixteen.

MAGOO: Don't be telling lies. You're only fifteen.

BILLY: (*Grabs bottle*) You didn't have to tell him that.
DAN: Do you still go to school?
BILLY: That's only for kids. (*Drinks.*) They learn you nothing there, only a lot of oul rubbish. I can't be bothered with that. Not now when there's a war on and a job to do, when every man has to do his duty. The future of our country is at stake.
MAGOO: You tell him. He knows his catechism all right. You recite for him.

(BILLY *comes to attention. Hands bottle to* MAGOO. *Marches round* DAN, *chants, complete with football-type hand-claps.*)

BILLY: Fuck the Pope. Kill the Taigs. Fenians out. Remember 1690. Glorious and Immortal Memory. Civil and Religious Liberty. No Pope Here.
(*Sings to tune of 'Wandering Star'.*)
If guns were made for shooting
Then skulls were made to crack.
You never saw a better Taig
Than with a bullet in his back.
I was born under a Union Jack, a Union, Union Jack.

Up the UVF. Tartan rules OK. Ulster will fight
and Ulster will be right. No surrender.
MAGOO: What do you think of that?
DAN: If he grows up a bit he could double for King Kong.
BILLY: (*Thumps him in the back*) Fuck you.
MAGOO: Leave him alone.

(BILLY *wanders around.* DAN *strains to hear upstairs.*)

BILLY: It's a big room, you could put our whole house in here.
MAGOO: What are you looking at?
DAN: Nothing. I'm blind.

(BILLY *finds medical samples, brings one to* MAGOO.)

BILLY: Hey, what's these. Can you read that label.
MAGOO: (*Peering*) Ah. . . .
BILLY: Jesus, you're near blind.
MAGOO: You might as well be, you can't read.
BILLY: I can so. What does it say?
MAGOO: They're drugs.

BILLY: The dirty bugger.
MAGOO: Not sex drugs. They're tranquillizers.
BILLY: (*opening bottle*) Them's the colour my mother takes. Do you want one?
MAGOO: No. We're soldiers.
BILLY: I'll keep these. What else is there? (*Opens another.*) What are these red ones?
DAN: That's streptomycin.
MAGOO: What's that when it's at home?
DAN: It's an antibiotic. Discovered by Selman Waksman.
BILLY: A Jewboy?
DAN: Does that matter?
MAGOO: Depends if he was a Protestant or a Catholic Jew.
DAN: Have you ever heard of him?
BILLY: Why would I?
DAN: Do you want to know how he discovered it?
BILLY: Why not?
DAN: He was looking in a pile of horseshit.
BILLY: You're pulling my leg.
DAN: He wanted to find out what was in it that made plants grow. And among a lot of other microbes he found one that prevented the growth of destructive ones. He didn't do much about it at the time, until the war came.
BILLY: What war?
DAN: The Second World War.
BILLY: I've seen that on TV.
DAN: They got all the scientists together, because in the First War disease had killed more people than the war. The year after that war ended twenty-one million people died of flu.
MAGOO: Flu?
DAN: There was no cure for pneumonia, meningitis, tuberculosis, typhoid, blood-poisoning, a lot of others. So another war got the scientists together and Selman Waksman remembered this microbe and it became one of the first antibiotics, and together with penicillin and the sulpha-drugs they wiped some of the greatest killers in history off the earth. You can now be cured of a disease that would have killed your grandfather in a few days and not even take time off work.

MAGOO: We're not here to listen to a lecture.

DAN: Fleming and Florey and Chain and Waksman and a host of others. We name no streets after them, we set no special days aside. I peddle them for a company with headquarters in a tax-free haven. To help you grow up strong to march on a public holiday to celebrate a little queer King who led a slaughter in 1690.

BILLY: I'm going to kill him.

MAGOO: What's that out the window, Billy?

BILLY: Where?

(BILLY *comes down front to where windows would be. Jumps back.*)

Holy Jesus, there's somebody coming in.

(MAGOO *grabs* DAN *and puts a hand over his mouth.*)

It's a woman. She just got out of a wee car. There's a man with her. What'll we do?

MAGOO: Hold him.

BILLY: (*Grabbing* DAN) What are you doing?

MAGOO: Getting my hood on.

(MAGOO *puts balaclava over his head, forgetting his glasses.*)

Oh fuck.

(MAGOO *rips hood off again as* BILLY *struggles with* DAN.)

BILLY: Jesus, let's run.

MAGOO: Get him in the kitchen. We'll put our hoods on there. Come on.

(MAGOO *and* BILLY *lift the chair with* DAN *in it and run into the kitchen.* LIZ *and* BOYD *enter from the hall. He carries a briefcase. She looks around.*)

LIZ: (*Calling*) Dan? Dan?

(LIZ *goes and puts her coat in the cloakroom beside the kitchen.*)

He can't be here.

BOYD: His car has gone.

LIZ: He and Michael will have gone for a drink. I was sure they would. Especially when the telephone wasn't answered. Well. We're safe.

(LIZ *picks up whiskey bottle, looks at level, sighs.*)

Do you want a drink?

BOYD: Please.

(LIZ *hands* BOYD *the bottle. Moves towards the kitchen.*)

LIZ: Would you like some ice?

BOYD: No, I won't bother.

(BOYD *pours a drink. Glass he previously used.*)

LIZ: Why are you being so mysterious?

BOYD: Am I?

LIZ: Why call me up? Why do you want to make sure we'll be alone.

(BOYD *puts down drink, lifts briefcase and takes out a revolver.*)

BOYD: This. I've done it.

LIZ: What?

BOYD: I had to. I thought it couldn't go on any longer.

LIZ: What? Boyd, what have you done?

(*There is a banging from the yard. The gate.*)

BOYD: What was that?

LIZ: Shall I look?

BOYD: (*Waving the gun loosely*) Yes.

(LIZ *goes to the glass doors and looks out.*)

LIZ: It's the back gate, it's banging. It must be kids. They're always running up and down there. I'll go and close it, shall I?

BOYD: (*Gun still pointed at her*) Leave it.

(LIZ *and* BOYD *stand, tense, looking at each other.*)

LIZ: Boyd, what is it?

BOYD: Will you take this away from me, please?

LIZ: I don't want to touch it.

BOYD: Please.

(LIZ *comes to* BOYD, *takes the gun carefully. He heaves a great sigh, sits down, takes a drink.* LIZ *puts the gun down.*)

BOYD: Thank you. It's like having a permanent erection. I was nearly going to ask you to take your clothes off.

LIZ: In this light? Wait till it's dark.

BOYD: Every fantasy you have becomes possible.

LIZ: How long have you had this?

BOYD: I went down at the beginning of the week and got it, got the permit and all, for my protection, after the threats. Not for myself, for my family, for their protection. That's how I justified it. I've been carrying it around and nobody knows I have it. I sit in the office, walk down the street, and nobody knows I'm carrying a gun. It has made me feel dirty . . . and powerful. That's why I wanted you to take it away from me.

LIZ: Have you . . .?

BOYD: No.

(BOYD *takes a drink.* LIZ *sits beside him.*)

I've wanted to use it. I'm aware of it every minute. Like everybody else here I've got used to the fact that you can't know your enemy, they could be sitting beside you in the bus. Nothing to make him different from you, except what he hides. I've been hiding that. And everybody has become my enemy.

LIZ: Didn't it make you feel safer?

BOYD: No. If you have a gun, you have to be prepared to use it, and if you are prepared to use it, then you end up just waiting for the chance, the need to use it. I look at everybody I meet, deciding whether I will have to shoot them.

LIZ: It would be self-defence.

BOYD: It would be failure, absolute failure. I would become the very thing I so detest. I didn't start working in politics for that. It seems like a century ago, but it's only seven years. When it seemed as if the old rotten machine was breaking down, when at last we could leave the past behind. I was marching for people, with people, ordinary people with ordinary but urgent problems—how to get a vote, a job, a decent house without having to be the right religion or know the right councillor. Demanding that things should be fair, should be seen to be fair, let's have some justice here, let's be rid of the old sectarian tango. It isn't just a question of which God rules OK? It is about how a few people used that to oppress, to promote ignorance for their own advantage. It seemed simple when thousands of ordinary people sat down in Derry in the pouring rain, without violence. They should have been irresistible, because their case was irresistible, and their decency should have been irresistible. But the bastards clobbered them. The cages were ready all the time. And the ordinary people melted away and the blind men took the field to make a place not fit to live in. I was wrong, history was too strong. And now I'm useless because I haven't the stomach to take up a gun. I'm left to contemplate the fact that politics is now a business for men who so lack imagination or a moral sense that they can order men out to kill and sleep easy in their beds. That seems to come within God's order, but it doesn't come within mine.

LIZ: What will happen to us?

BOYD: I feel as if I have a disease, or, even worse, that I always had a disease dormant in me, and that I've let it out.

LIZ: There must be a cure.

BOYD: Dan and his tranquillizers, half the population on the happy pills. That's no cure.

LIZ: I will have a drink.

BOYD: (*Getting up*) I'll get you a glass.

(BOYD *moves towards kitchen.*)

LIZ: There's one here.

(BOYD *gets a glass from a shelf, pours them both drinks.*)

BOYD: We have a disease, a plague.

LIZ: The Black Death.

BOYD: Ordinary treatment doesn't work. So you resort to the knife, try an exploratory operation, cut out some offending part. That doesn't work. So cut deeper, cut the tripes out of the body. But there is no single malignant growth, it spreads and spreads, and it's infectious.

LIZ: We do like they used to do with smallpox, we isolate it.

BOYD: Right. Intern the known germ carriers.

LIZ: We know that doesn't work.

BOYD: Then intern the lot. Not just fever hospitals, but find an island and keep everybody on it.

LIZ: We have the island.

BOYD: This disease drives people mad and they attack each other.

LIZ: Tranquillize them.

BOYD: Put guards around the border. For the healthy ones, prescribe a change of air, and help them to get out. For the rest, give them a few quid, a prison governor, let him run it with the help of the trusty prisoners, knowing they'll be the biggest gangsters, then wait for the disease or the people to die out. Do I describe a familiar policy?

LIZ: But you must go on looking for a cure?

BOYD: Why? Nobody else thinks they suffer from our disease. Why waste money?

LIZ: There must be an answer somewhere. The trouble with ignorance is that it doesn't allow us to know how ignorant we are.

BOYD: Doctor John Snow.

LIZ: Who was he?

BOYD: Dan told me about him. They had a cholera plague in London about a hundred years ago. People were dying like flies. Nobody knew what to do. It was at its worst in one particular place, and they were so desperate that they advertised, in the papers, for anybody who could cure them. Well, they got all kinds of nutters. Then John Snow came along and said—Take the handle off the pump in the street. They thought he was another nut, but they were desperate enough to try. The plague stopped. John Snow had no visions, no little voices, no theories, no technology. All he did was walk about the streets, looking, with clear eyes. He saw that in the local poorhouse the inmates might be starving but they weren't ill. Why? Because they had their own well. But I'm as blind as anyone else, I don't know where to look. What a bloody mess, eh? I go out and get myself a gun.

LIZ: I have the gun. You gave it to me.

BOYD: Thank you. What will you do?

LIZ: Did you really want me to take my clothes off?

BOYD: (*Embarrassed*) Yes.

LIZ: Well. I think loving is what I do best. Let's go to bed.

BOYD: I surrender.

LIZ: You go upstairs, I'll follow you.

(LIZ *rises, gives* BOYD *a swift kiss.* BOYD *exits. She tidies the glasses. Wonders what to do with the gun then puts it back in the briefcase, leaving it open. Goes upstairs.*

DAN *enters from the kitchen, still blindfolded, taking the rope off his hands. He listens. Takes the blindfold off. Sees gun. He walks down front to the phone, has his hand out to lift it, when he doubles up in agony.)*

DAN: Ohhh, I have to have a piss. (*Looks at ceiling.*) I suppose I could use the sink.

(MAC *appears at the glass doors, panting, harassed, holding machine-gun, hood half-off, his only real disguise dark glasses. Comes in through doors.*)

MAC: I'm behind you, friend, rest easy. Where the hell are the other two? What happened here?

DAN: One night in Birdland, Parker and his band were due on stage. Parker was very sick, it was near the end of his tolerance of life. Bud Powell came on first and he was so sick and so drunk that he could hardly sit at the piano. All alone he began to play a tune called 'Little Willie leaps'.

MAC: I don't want to hear this shit. Where are they?

DAN: The band came on then and set up and Parker called the first number, a tune called 'Hallucination'. Powell played 'Little Willie Leaps'. The band stopped, began again. Powell played 'Little Willie Leaps'. Then these two great musicians cursed each other and Powell staggered off the stand. Bird stepped up to the microphone and with an angry heart he called out 'Bud Powell'. Fourteen times he called his name while gradually all the people left.

MAC: Where are they?

DAN: They ran away.

MAC: (*Throwing down keys*) There's your car keys. Change the number plates, the Taigs'll be after it. And don't say nothing. I know your wife, I know your child. Remember I'm doing this for you. Have you got a gun here? Give it to me.

DAN: I haven't got one.

MAC: You people make me sick. You won't do nothing for yourselves, you haven't the stomach for it. You wait for us to clean up the mess. You failed so you headed the ball to us. And when we've done the job you'll say, thanks very much, now fuck off.

(BERTHA *appears at the glass door behind him. Creeps forward during speech looking for something to hit* MAC *with.*)

You look down on us, you think we're dirt, you think we

should go on doing what we're told. Well, it's too late now, we're not wee boys any more, we won't be used. If nobody else will run this country, we will run it. Give me a gun.

DAN: You have one.

MAC: I jammed this with the second burst I put into them, them animals.

(BERTHA *hits* MAC *over the head with a flower vase and knocks him out.* DAN *swings round.*)

DAN: Bertha!

BERTHA: Do you think I've killed him?

DAN: I hope not.

BERTHA: I hope I have.

DAN: He had my car.

BERTHA: Listen, I came round to tell you. A fella and a girl have just been to my door asking after your car. I sent them off and ran round here.

DAN: Looking for me?

BERTHA: Phone the police, Dan.

(*Loud rattle of front door knocker.*)

That might be them.

DAN: Bertha, run, use your phone.

BERTHA: Suppose he wakens up, who'll watch him?

DAN: Just go.

BERTHA: You could be caught between the both of them. I'll answer the door.

DAN: Bertha, don't get mixed up in this, look after yourself.

BERTHA: I will not. You think I'm afraid of them? You don't know me. You take care of him, I'll see to them. Sure it might be anybody. I can look after myself. I was a goalkeeper at hockey.

(BERTHA *goes out.* DAN *grabs* MAC *and shoves him into the cloakroom. Then shoves the gun behind a chair.*)

DAN: Ohh, I've got to have a pee.

(DAN *grabs up a metal wastebasket and gets his penis out. At that moment* BERTHA *enters backwards with a young girl,* UNA, *holding a gun on her.* UNA *in denim. Followed by a weedy lad in wide trousers at half-mast and boots,* SEAN. *He closes the living-room door.*)

UNA: Hold it.
SEAN: Put that weapon away. There's ladies present.
DAN: I accept the historical decline of capitalism, I even wish for its speedy end, and with it the bourgeois sense of property. Nevertheless this is my house and if I want to pee in it, I will.
SEAN: Not in the front room.
DAN: Nothing can stop me.
(DAN *turns away and we hear the ringing sound of him gushing into the metal basket. Finishes, zips himself up, puts basket down.*)
SEAN: I ought to plug you.
BERTHA: You little squirt, get out of this house.
SEAN: Shut up, missus.
UNA: (*Commanding*) Leave this to me. Is that your car down the back of here?
DAN: I don't know.
(UNA *tosses down a box of drug samples.*)
UNA: A car full of drugs?
SEAN: (*Pointing*) There's more of them here.
BERTHA: Now listen, young woman, we are respectable people....
SEAN: Just shut up, missus.
BERTHA: You pathetic wee scrap, I'd put you over my knee and skelp you. It's what your mother should have done long ago.
UNA: Is there anybody upstairs?
DAN: No, no one, no one upstairs.
UNA: Sean, look in the kitchen.
SEAN: You tell her not to talk to me like that.
(SEAN *goes into the kitchen.*)
UNA: Two people are dead. Your car was used.
DAN: I'm sorry.
UNA: I'll bet you are.
BERTHA: The car was stolen and he has reported it to the police. They'll be here any minute so you two just scram.
(SEAN *comes back.*)
SEAN: Nothing in the kitchen.
UNA: Sit down.
(BERTHA *and* DAN *sit on the couch.*)

Who did it?

DAN: I had nothing to do with it.

UNA: You let it happen.

BERTHA: What do you expect from him?

UNA: Where's the big man who took the car?

BERTHA: He's not here. He's gone.

UNA: Who was he?

BERTHA: We never saw his face.

UNA: Is that right?

DAN: I didn't know him.

UNA: How long is he gone?

DAN: Not long.

UNA: Sean, see what you can find.

(SEAN *begins to look around.*)

DAN: The TV isn't insured.

UNA: We're not thieves.

BERTHA: What are you then?

UNA: Soldiers.

BERTHA: More like scum off the streets.

SEAN: Just shut up, missus.

BERTHA: It would take a better man than you, sonny boy.

DAN: Will you let her go? She knows nothing.

SEAN: (*With drug samples*) Hey, he's got the wee blue ones. Do you want one?

UNA: No.

(SEAN *takes one.*)

DAN: Will you let her go?

SEAN: That big bitch would go straight to a phone.

BERTHA: It's as well you're sheltering behind a gun, you wee fart. And a girl at that. What do you two think you'll achieve here, trying to frighten innocent, respectable people? We have nothing to do with your dirty wee war. No decent people have.

UNA: You are wrong.

BERTHA: Count the votes you got, any election you like.

UNA: Look at the people you voted in. Is that the best democracy can do? Well, I can do without it.

BERTHA: It proves you were never wanted.

UNA: The Catholic people were attacked. They needed us. We haven't failed them. We have the right to defend ourselves.

BERTHA: By planting bombs? Dear, you're going the wrong way about it.

UNA: We are fighting oppression. For a new Ireland.

BERTHA: Do you seriously mean to stand there and tell me that you think the best way to persuade people to vote for your new Ireland is to bomb and kill them and their children? You really think they'd be more likely to agree with you after that?

UNA: It's a war. You attacked us first.

BERTHA: We did not.

UNA: Every day, every day of my life. My mother worked in a shirt factory. There was only work for women. My father never had a job. He fought for the Republican cause in the fifties, he was a marked man after that. Our streets were full of men with nowhere to go, all living off the women. When we left school we were told, emigrate, that's your only hope. We lived in slums, without votes, without hope, with no future. And when we protested they burned our houses down and said we had fired them ourselves. They caged us up, tortured us, violated us. We'll never stop fighting, because it's better no future than the one we had. Better to destroy everything because it wasn't worth having in the first place. And if we have to we will wrap ourselves in dynamite and walk through the ring of steel.

(SEAN *is about to look in the briefcase.*)

DAN: Are you going to kill us now?

UNA: If we have to.

(DAN *stands up, which distracts* SEAN.)

Sit down.

DAN: Does it matter if I die standing up or sitting down?

UNA: Sit down.

DAN: It doesn't matter to me.

UNA: I said I would kill you if I have to.

DAN: You will decide.

UNA: It won't give me any pleasure.

DAN: That's a relief. It's all a great relief. Here's me has been worrying about making choices, decisions, balancing rights and wrongs, freedom and law, and I needn't bother. You will decide. Do I have a last request?

UNA: Sit down.

DAN: Let's make love.

UNA: What?

SEAN: You watch your mouth.

DAN: Let us make love. It's the only weapon I've got.

UNA: Sit down.

(DAN *opens his trousers, begins to undress.*)

DAN: Bertha, what's the last thing you'd like to do before you die?

BERTHA: Make love.

DAN: Care to join me?

UNA: Sean, do something.

BERTHA: He'll not be much use to me.

(BERTHA *also gets up and begins to strip.*)

Come here, son.

UNA: Stop it.

DAN: What's your name?

UNA: Stop this.

SEAN: Una, Una, do something.

DAN: Una. I'm Dan, I'm pleased to meet you. It's a pleasure to know the name of the person who will decide if I die. Of course you may shoot me because my prick is too small, I'll have to take the chance. Stick around and shoot my daughter when she comes home for painting snowballs red.

(*Both* DAN *and* BERTHA *still stripping, teasing. Most of her clothes end up in the Wendy House.*)

BERTHA: (*Removing her bra*) How does that grab you?

SEAN: These two are mad.

DAN: I was afraid while I thought I would die because of something I did, there would be some reason. But if I may die for no reason then I will live the way I please. All I want to do is love you, Una.

UNA: No.

DAN: Are you afraid of me?

(UNA *points the gun at him and fires. It misfires. She begins to weep with rage as she struggles with the gun.*)

BERTHA: You tried to kill him.

SEAN: Oh Jesus.

(SEAN *tries to run, but mistakes the doors and tries to run out by way of the cloakroom. He recoils from it when he opens the door.*)

My God, there's a dead man in there. Run, Una, run.

(SEAN *flees out by the open glass door.* UNA *sobbing hurls the gun at* DAN *and runs out the front.* BERTHA *has half-chased* SEAN *and is round the back of the couch.* DAN *kicks the gun under the couch and goes round to look in the cloakroom.*)

BERTHA: Is he still breathing?

DAN: Yes.

BERTHA: So are you, thank God.

DAN: Yes. Yes, I am.

BERTHA: Lock that door.

(BERTHA *goes to the roofless Wendy House for her clothes.* DAN *turns the key in cloakroom door and joins her. They stand half-naked, only seen from waist up.*)

Let's call the police.

DAN: I suppose we should.

BERTHA: Do you know, I'm all excited.

DAN: So am I, Bertha, for the first time in six months. I can feel it.

BERTHA: (*Reaches down to touch him*) So can I.

DAN: I'll phone them in a minute. Bird lives.

BERTHA: Right.

(DAN *and* BERTHA *kiss. Sink down. A pause.*
Enter CAROL *from upstairs, putting on her coat, ready to go. Followed by a distraught* MICHAEL.)

MICHAEL: Where are you going?

CAROL: Home.

MICHAEL: Why?

CAROL: You know why.

MICHAEL: I was tired. I'd had too much to drink last night.

CAROL: It wasn't my fault.

MICHAEL: I didn't say it was.

CAROL: You as much as did.

MICHAEL: I didn't mean that.
CAROL: What did you mean then?
MICHAEL: I just asked what you were afraid of?
CAROL: Nothing.
MICHAEL: You were so tense.
CAROL: You're the one that's afraid.
MICHAEL: Please don't go.
CAROL: You said you'd give me money.
MICHAEL: Oh, yes.

(*While* MICHAEL *fumbles out the money* DAN *and* BERTHA *peer over, then duck down.*)

CAROL: You should have told me. You took advantage of me.
MICHAEL: I didn't.
CAROL: You did.
MICHAEL: I didn't.
CAROL: Just because I didn't want to go home.
MICHAEL: I didn't.
CAROL: I never meant to do it.
MICHAEL: We didn't do it.

(*The heads pop up and down again.*)

CAROL: Whose fault was that?
MICHAEL: Nobody's.
CAROL: It wasn't mine.
MICHAEL: You could have helped me.
CAROL: What sort of girl do you think I am?

(BERTHA*'s head pops up, pulled down.*)

MICHAEL: For God's sake.
CAROL: I thought you'd be different.
MICHAEL: How?
CAROL: I don't know. Well, I'm away.
MICHAEL: Please, don't go. Please. Let's try again.

(*Heads pop up.*)

CAROL: Now?
MICHAEL: No.
CAROL: I have to go.
MICHAEL: I want a child.
CAROL: You'd be the first in medical history.
MICHAEL: Let's not be afraid.

CAROL: Afraid of what? You're married. That's something you didn't tell me first.

MICHAEL: I've left my wife.

CAROL: Didn't you have any children by her?

MICHAEL: No.

CAROL: Is that why you left her?

MICHAEL: It was her fault.

CAROL: But you can't even do it.

(*Michael is nearly hysterical.*)

MICHAEL: I have to know there is a future. Not just going blindly down the burning tunnel with its dead and pitch dark end.

CAROL: A future with me?

MICHAEL: Yes.

CAROL: What's my name?

MICHAEL: Carol.

CAROL: What's my other name?

MICHAEL: I . . . don't remember. I came here . . . to say there was a better world. I came here to save you.

CAROL: You'll find us very hard to save. I'll be late for my train.

(CAROL *moves to door.* MICHAEL *blocks her.* BERTHA *and* DAN *duck down.*)

MICHAEL: I have all this love. I have to have something to live for.

CAROL: It wasn't my fault. You know more than me.

(CAROL *goes out, by way of kitchen.* MICHAEL *bows his head, near tears.*

DAN *and* BERTHA *pop up, uncertain what to do. Hear someone, duck down.*

Enter BOYD *from upstairs, wearing only* DAN'*s dressing-gown. Stops shocked.*)

BOYD: Oh. Michael.

MICHAEL: What are you doing here?

BOYD: I'm . . . I'm . . . going to make a cup of coffee, just a cup of coffee. I thought you were out having a drink.

MICHAEL: No.

BOYD: Then where's Dan?

MICHAEL: I don't know.

BOYD: Haven't you seen him?

MICHAEL: He was here.
BOYD: Here? When? Now?
MICHAEL: Some time ago.
BOYD: I wonder where he is.
MICHAEL: Why?
BOYD: Ah . . . because.
MICHAEL: What?
BOYD: You know . . .
MICHAEL: That's his dressing-gown.
BOYD: Yes.
MICHAEL: You're wearing his dressing-gown.
BOYD: Yes.
MICHAEL: Where's Liz?
BOYD: Michael it was like this. . . .
MICHAEL: Where is she?
BOYD: Upstairs.
MICHAEL: Upstairs.
BOYD: In bed. You see . . . it's a long story. . . .
MICHAEL: (*A scream*) Aaahhh.
BOYD: Now hang on, Michael . . .
MICHAEL: Why you?
BOYD: It just happened.
MICHAEL: It should have been me.
BOYD: Why you?
MICHAEL: I flew here at once, flew, immediately, to take her away with me.
BOYD: What?
MICHAEL: I came here to help, to do the right thing, to help. I came from England to help.
BOYD: Help who?
MICHAEL: She asked me. To take her, to take the child. To save them. I came.
BOYD: Michael, catch yourself on.
MICHAEL: And now . . . why won't she let me help her?
BOYD: I don't know.
MICHAEL: Why you?
BOYD: I don't matter. It was just friendly.
MICHAEL: Why can't I help?

BOYD: Michael, I'm going to make some coffee. Do you want some?

MICHAEL: What's wrong with me?

BOYD: Nothing.

MICHAEL: I've nowhere to go. I can't go back. I am burning. Burning and burning and burning blind. Burning. I am devoured. My root is blasted away. I don't recognize the streets. I don't recognize the faces. I have no place left. You have destroyed it, taken it from me. Ah. Ah. Ah.

(*Howling*, MICHAEL *flings himself on* BOYD *who topples over with him on top.* DAN *springs round and pulls him off.* BERTHA *takes* MICHAEL *in her arms and quietens him.*)

BERTHA: There, there, it's all right, it's all right now. He needs a doctor.

DAN: You look after him. I thought this was going to be the funny bit. Are you all right?

BOYD: Yes. Where were you?

DAN: In the Wendy House.

BOYD: All the time?

DAN: Not all the time.

BOYD: So you know.

DAN: Yes. I know.

BOYD: I don't know what to say.

DAN: Then don't say anything. Go and make the coffee. That's what happens next. I'm going to play my Parker record which was interrupted some time ago.

BOYD: What's been going on?

DAN: It's over now. We'll survive. Make the coffee.

(DAN *goes to stereo.*)

BOYD: Dan. Nothing happened. We didn't. I had the intention. But. I'm very tired. I'm sorry.

DAN: Go on.

BOYD: I think I'll get dressed first, I'll feel more comfortable.

DAN: No, make some sweet tea for him.

BOYD: OK.

(BOYD *goes to kitchen.* BERTHA *gets* MICHAEL *to sit with her on the couch. He is drained, vacant.*)

BERTHA: You come and sit down, that's right. You're all right.

DAN: How is he?

BERTHA: I think he'll survive.

(DAN *puts on 'Crazeology', loud. Looks up at ceiling, knowing the sound will tell* LIZ *he is there. He dances a little to the record.*)

DAN: Thanks, Bertha.

BERTHA: Don't mention it. It's easier when you know what you're afraid of. I've been afraid of being frightened.

DAN: We've all been afraid to live. For fear of what might happen. Well, not any more. Charlie Parker, did you forgive Bud Powell before you died? I'm sure you did.

(LIZ, *in gown, enters.* DAN, *turns down music. Looks stern.*)

LIZ: Hello, Dan.

DAN: Hello.

LIZ: So you know.

DAN: I know.

LIZ: So?

DAN: I think it's disgusting. Under my roof in my own bed. Well, my girl, you have made your bed and now you will have to lie in it. You can follow your fancy man, although, mark my words, he will not want you after he has got what he wants.

LIZ: Oh no.

DAN: You can pack your bags and go.

LIZ: Give me another chance.

DAN: How dare you behave like a person instead of a wife?

(DAN *breaks up in laughter. Holds his arms out.*)

Come here.

(LIZ *comes into* DAN'*s arms.*)

Let's start again. Together.

LIZ: Let's. What have you two been up to? What's been going on?

DAN: This and that, nothing much.

LIZ: What happened to Michael?

DAN: We're very hard to save.

LIZ: And where's Boyd?

DAN: In the kitchen making coffee.

LIZ: (*Breaking away, moving towards kitchen*) Is he . . .?

DAN: We're all together.

(*With a tearing crash* MAC *bursts the lock on the cloakroom door and tumbles out.*

DAN *grabs up the jammed machine-gun from behind the chair.*

BERTHA *gets the pistol which misfired from under the couch.*

LIZ *grabs up* BOYD'*s gun out of the briefcase.*

In the face of this artillery MAC *turns up his eyes.*)

MAC: Oh Jesus.

(MAC *faints.*)

LIZ: Dan, Dan, I pulled the trigger, I pulled the trigger and nothing happened. Oh God, I pulled the trigger, before I thought.

DAN: The safety catch. (*Calls*) Boyd.

(BOYD, *the gown open and flapping round him, exposing his vulnerability, runs out of the kitchen. There is a shot behind him and he is flung forward.*

UNA, *with a gun, appears behind him.* SEAN *appears at the glass door, which is open.*)

SEAN: That's him, that's the one, and that's the one I saw in the cupboard, him on the floor, the man we're looking for.

DAN: Stand still.

(UNA *and* SEAN *freeze in the face of the guns.*)

Why? Why did you kill him?

UNA: I had him in the kitchen and he ran.

DAN: Put down your gun.

UNA: Sean has a solicitor's name in his pocket. We claim the right to a fair trial and political prisoner status in the event of any future amnesty.

SEAN: And compensation in the event of criminal injury, and the right not to be tortured under the Commission of Human Rights.

DAN: Put down the gun.

(MICHAEL *begins to howl, he gets up and runs towards* UNA.)

BERTHA: He's not got his wits, he doesn't know what he's doing.

DAN: Liz.

(*As* SEAN *grabs* MICHAEL *for a shield,* DAN *drops the jammed machine-gun and* LIZ *throws him* BOYD'*s gun.*)

Down.

(LIZ *and* BERTHA *crouch on our side of the couch.* DAN *has the pistol pointed, arm at full stretch, supported by the left hand, a trained position.*

SEAN *and* UNA *shelter behind the howling* MICHAEL.)

SEAN: Just let us go, mister.

(MAC *rises up from behind the couch, dazed.*)

MAC: What happened? What happened?

(MAC *is shot from behind by* UNA. SEAN *and* UNA *push* MICHAEL *away and run out the glass door.* MICHAEL *stops howling with the shot.*)

DAN: Michael, out of the way.

(DAN *steadies himself at the door and fires two shots. Two empty clicks.*)

Boyd, you never loaded it, you put no bullets in it.

(MAGOO *comes bursting through the living-room door. With his knife.*)

MAGOO: Everybody stand still so I can see you. I left my glasses here.

(BERTHA *lifts the bucket of piss and upends it over his head.* DAN *hurls the gun away from him.*)

DAN: Bud Powell, Bud Powell, Bud Powell, Bud Powell, Bud Powell. Bud Powell. Bud Powell. Bud Powell. Bud Powell. Bud Powell. Bud Powell. Bud Powell. Bud Powell. Bud Powell. . . .

(*Till* LIZ *puts her arms round* DAN *and silences him.*)

CURTAIN